History and Traditions of the Gonja

History and Traditions of the Gonja

by
J.A. Braimah
H.H. Tomlinson
and
Osafroadu Amankwatia

African Occasional Papers, No. 6

University of Calgary Press

© 1997 P.L. Shinnie. All rights reserved
ISBN 1-895176-38-7
ISSN 0832-8277

University of Calgary Press
2500 University Drive NW
Calgary, Alberta
Canada T2N 1N4

Canadian Cataloguing in Publication Data

Braimah, J.A.
    History and traditions of the Gonja

    (African occasional papers, ISSN 0832-8277 ; no. 6)
    Includes bibliographical references.
    ISBN 1-895176-38-7

    1. Gonja Region (Ghana)—History. 2. Gonja (African
    people)—History. 3. Gonja (African people)—Social life
    and customs. I. Tomlinson, H.H., 1924– II. Amankwatia,
    Osafroadu, 1915–1975. III. Title. IV. Series.
DT512.9.G65B72 1997   966.7   C97-910913-2

COMMITTED TO THE DEVELOPMENT OF CULTURE AND THE ARTS
Financial support provided in part by the Alberta Foundation for the Arts.

Printed and bound in Canada.
♾ This book is printed on acid-free paper.

Table of Contents

Editor's Introduction

The idea of a publication on the history and customs of the Gonja people of northern Ghana first came to me at Damongo on the occasion of the Damba festival on 11th December 1984, when the late J.A. Braimah, then Yagbumwura gave me a typescript of a history of his people that he had written and asked about the possibility of publishing it.

I accepted the charge and thought that with a commentary it would be suitable as one of the series of the University of Calgary African Occasional Papers. I passed the text to Professor Ivor Wilks of Northwestern University hoping that, as the best informed of historians of Gonja and being involved with his colleagues N. Levtzion and B. Haight in the editing and publishing of the important Arabic written material for Gonja history[1] he would produce a valuable commentary.

Some years later Wilks decided that the nature of Braimah's text made it difficult for him to do justice to it and withdrew from the project. As a result of this I decided to publish the text as it stood with minimal editing by myself. I much regret that the planned commentary and the more learned editing than I am capable of was not done but appreciate the reasons for the withdrawal.

It is clear that there are differences between the interpretation of Gonja history as given by a traditionally orientated native historian and that of modern scholars and the differences may provide interesting material for subsequent discussions. It should also be said that J.A. Braimah wrote other versions of the history of his people one of which was published by the Institute of African Studies of the University of Ghana in mimeographed form as "The Founding of the Gonja Empire" no date but possibly 1971.

---

1 Published as *Chronicles from Gonja. A tradition of West African Muslim historiography.* Cambridge University Press, 1986.

At about the same time that I received his text from J.A. Braimah, I became aware that Mr. H. Tomlinson, who had served in Gonja as a British District Officer in the 1950s had written an essay on the customs of the Gonja. This essay had been mimeographed and published, with a limited distribution, and without Mr. Tomlinson's knowledge, by the Institute of African Studies of the University of Ghana and it is now republished here, with minor editorial changes, with the permission of the author and of Professor Arhin, then director of that Institute.

The third document by Osafroadu Amankwatia also came into my hands at the same time and was given to me by J.A. Braimah (Yagbumwura Timu). Mr. Braimah subsequently wrote to me on 3 July 1985 saying of the document "Written by me. Submitted to Gonja Traditional Council, but rejected by Yagbumwura Ewuntuma. Mr. Osafroadu Amankwatia, who was counsel to the Northern Regional House of Chiefs, Tamale, came across it and improved on it by further research. He presented it to the Gonja Traditional Authority and this time it was accepted by the Gonja Traditional Council with some amendments." Mr. Braimah died on 26 January 1987.

Readers will notice some variation in spelling of proper names. I decided that this variation, such as "Yabumwura," or "Yagbumwura," or in the official spelling which Mr. Braimah introduced in 1985, "Yagbongwura," would not make for too much confusion, so spellings have been left as authors gave them.

Since this text was prepared for the press in 1992, a paper has been published by Esther and Jack Goody ("Creating a text: Alternate interpretations of Gonja drum histories," *Africa* 62 (1992): 266–70) in which important light is thrown on the drum histories on which J. A. Braiman relied heavily for his version of Gonja history. Readers of this publication will find the Goodys' paper a useful commentary on the use of drum histories.

P.L. Shinnie

A History of the Gonja State

by

J.A. Braimah, Yagbumwura

Preface

In 1972, I was requested by the members of the Voluntary Workshop Association of Ghana who worked on the Songhai resettlement to give them a talk on Gonja history. The students of the St. Charles Secondary School, Tamale, also visited me in Kpembe with one of their lecturers that same year and also made the same request. A third party was the students of the Salaga/Kpandai Local Authority Middle School, Kpembe.

This year (1973) the members of the Voluntary Workshop Association of Ghana who returned to continue their work on Songhai resettlement again requested me to talk to them on the history of Gonja.

Because of the interest shown by many people about the history of the Gonja people I decided to write this brief history of Gonja. The work covers the period from 1566/7 to 1711/12 during which time there was a struggle between two groups of Mandinka, the Manwura and his clan and the Lata Ngbanya whose leader was Lata (Lanta) Jakpa, for power. Ndewura Jakpa who is well known as the founder of Gonja was the son of Lata (Dii Ngoro) Jakpa.

Fragments of Gonja history have been written by European writers and translations of Arabic manuscripts have been made. The researches made into the history of the Gonja people by the researchers and the Institute of African Studies of the University of Ghana have been of considerable help. This is of course the first work on Gonja history that has been undertaken by a Gonja and the verses of the traditional drums have been quoted to support some of the facts given by oral traditions.

J.A.B.

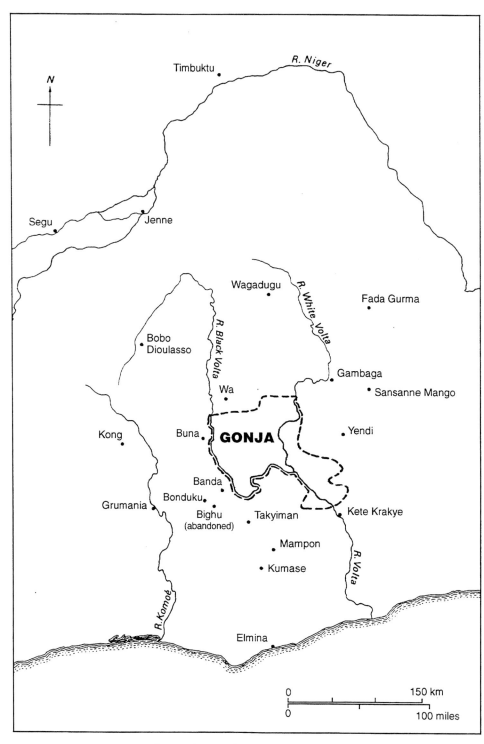

Map 1. Gonja: the regional setting.

Introduction

During the period of Colonial Administration those of us who went to school were made to learn only foreign history, most especially British history, and no one cared to teach us our own history. Of course, it was not so with our illiterate contemporaries; they were being taught our own local history by our elders and therefore had an advantage over us in this respect.

The old idea that tropical Africa can have no history in the conventional sense because it has no written documents is simply not true. If tropical Africa lacks a continuous sense of methodical record of public events and the study of growth of nations it does not lack a whole train of events connected with the past empires and states, their prominent kings or sovereigns and other things.

In the reconstruction of history where written records are absent, legend and folk tradition can be pieced together to form something of the historical picture of recent events. In Gonja we have the traditional drummers, the Kuntunkure and the Mbontokurbi drummers, who recite verses which give the history of the people most especially the exploits of the founder of the Gonja Empire, Ndewura Jakpa.

The exploits of distinguished leaders or kings and of individual families, as given by the drummers are, in many cases, the repetition of some well-worn saga, adding to it events in recent history, which contains a modicum of historical fact. The trouble with oral tradition is that it lacks chronology.

Gonja is one of the lucky tribes which has had its history recorded by Arab Muslims who accompanied them to this part of the world. According to Arabic manuscript and oral tradition, the Gonjas, who were originally Mandingo (Gonja Dingo-ebi), or Mandinka, migrated from the country of Mande, that is, from the Mali Empire, many years before the Hejra Year 1000.

One of the oldest surviving documents written in an African language is the Isnad of Al-Haji Muhamed from about A.D. 1736, a Gonja

History written in Arabic with its first item referring to A.D. 1585, though of course, there are earlier European texts.

Mande is a state within the Mali Empire in the Sudan.

> The Sudan Zone may be divided into three historical regions: Senegalese Chieftaincies, Soninke and Mandinka states between the Niger and Senegal, and the Songhay region of Upper Niger; all of which, together with central Mande peoples, were embraced within the sphere of the Empire of Mali. These historical regions correspond to the main linguistic regions: West Atlantic (Serer, Wolof, Fulbe, and Tokolor), Mande (Soninke and Mandinka), and the isolated Songhay language.[1]

Gonja historians claim that their royal residence in Mande is Kaaba (Kangaba). "Kangaba which has always been the ritual centre of state and people, where there is a sanctuary where septennial cult ceremonies, which draw together representatives of the various Mande peoples are still held."[2]

The Gonja war song is called "Sin bo aya"; the meaning is "The Sin migrates." From the expression one would assume that the original home of the Gonjas is Sin, one of the Mande states to be found in Senegal.

The Gonja war song is as follows:

> The Sin migrates,
> We are the Mbongwurana [war Captains].
> The Sin migrators, wanderers in [other] countries.
> The Sin migrators,
> Today here it is:
> Disturbed Sin migrators.
> The lads say they would fight,
> Disturbed Sin migrators.
> Cummerbunds are now around their knees;
> The lasses say they would fight,
> Disturbed Sin migrators.
> The loin-cloth is around their knees,
> Sin migrators,
> Disturbed Sin migrators,
> The sound of the *agangang* drums are heard approaching;
> Sin migrators.

The Kpembe and Tuluwe Gonjas are referred to as the "Singbing-ebi," that is, the "Sin protectors or barriers" and the "Singbingwura" of

---

1 J. Spencer Trimingham, *A History of West Africa* (London: Oxford University Press, 1945), p. 65.

2 Op. cit., p. 65.

Kpembe's *ntunpana* appellation, which is the appellation of all Chiefs of Singbing is:

Asante kotoko	The porcupine of Ashanti
[versus]	
Singbinghene, brimpon	The Sin barring king, the great
Wo na wa hwe ase	It is he who when he falls
Na mpanini ba wu	The elders will die
okum apem	You kill a thousand [of his men]
Na apem beba	And a thousand will come [as reinforcement].

The Singbing family are the direct descendants or close relatives of Ndewura Jakpa. Another Gonja *ntunpana* drum appellation is:[3]

Kotoko Sin bra du	The porcupine of Sin who brought a retinue
Sin bra du	The Sin with a retinue
Amankwa	And servant of the state
Wo fro dua	If you intend to climb a tree
Wa hwe ase a	If you then fall
Na ya ma wu due	You will be sympathized with

Three Gonja proverbs refer to the Sin; they are:

1. Binypo luwe.	The learned [people]
N'Sin-ba e la anyi	We are half Sins [now]
2. Sin,kra 'nu	Sin, hear again;
Eseng-iipo ni kafong ko	It is an informer who worries.
3. Sin Bey niya ?	[What about] the Sin sovereign's (Bey) share?
Fa la dimadi	If you call your-self a person,
A mink ba yuu so	And you have no one to rely on,
Esi jigo e la fo	You are a foolish person.

The Gonjas were in the Songhay Empire and were known to have been at Dza, Jenne, Gao (Kawkaw), Fio, Say and Sengu.

The Mbontokurbi travelling song of the Gonja leader Lata (Lanta) Jakpa is:

---

3 This verse is in the Twi language, as are many drum verses current in Gonja. The trans-lations are not literal, but give the general sense. It should be noted that "Amankwa" is a personal name – *ed.*

A stranger (toure) but he reigned;
Challenge to Manwu
He is forceful (kankang); but he reigned
Challenge to Manwu.
The hunting [warrior] king.
He again licks, and splashes away.
I am Dii Ngoro Jakpa,
The warrior king
Who follows the war trails.
Which people surrendered to an alien powerful prince?
It was the people of Gbirbi who surrendered to an alien powerful prince.
Which people surrendered to an alien powerful prince?
It was the people of Kachari who surrendered to an alien powerful prince.
He is the invading confiscator
The warrior leader (lan kpang)
He is the great solitary wasp;
He captures princes and turns them into slaves
And captures slaves
And turns them into princes
Behold the king who ascended hills [other sovereigns]
On his advance.
A wise man has to live with fools.
A stone does not walk
But it rolls.

Further evidence of the Gonja having come from the far West is to be found in the titles of kings (chiefs) in the West Coast of the Atlantic and north Africa such as "Burba" and "Bey" used in the Kuntunkure and Mbontokurbi drum verses. "Fari" and "Si," which are titles of kings in the former Songhay Empire are also used in the drum verses.

"Bur-ba" is found in the Kuntunkure verses entitled "K'Borichulo," meaning "In Praise of God" in the stanza:

Mbong-bi Mo-ano so nchu
N ya sa Lanta Bur-ba;
Ne e so m bulo ngbine
A dese.

Meaning:

The streams [lieutenants] at the Mo boundary
Should confiscate the water [sovereignty]
And vest it in Lanta the Bur-ba
And he will fill his heart
And lie down.

Early Portuguese travellers show that by the middle of the fifteenth century the *damel* of Kojor, and *barak* of Wula, the *ten* of Baol, and the "bur-bar-Salum" were independent of the "bur-bar-Jolof," although they recognised him a *suzerain* and would seek his aid as arbitrator.[4]

"Bur" alone, without the "ba," is also used as the title of king as in the Gonja titles "Bur Wura," "Bur Manwura," "Bur Lannyo," and "Bur Kpembewura."[5]

"Bey," which is the title of a native ruler of Tunis, is found in the Gonja title "Manwule Bey-so" "The sovereign (Bey) trapper of Manwule and in 'Bey-so-bi'—The junior Bey (Sovereign) trapper" in the Kuntunkure drum verse "Manwul Bey-so."

"Dey," which was the title of a governor of Algiers before the French conquest of 1830 and formerly the title of a ruler of Tunis of Tripoli is found in the Gonja titles "Mo-Dey" (Mo sovereign) and "Wang-Dey" (Dagomba sovereign) in the Kuntunkure and Mbontokurbi drum verses.

"Fari" and "fa" (abbreviation of "fari") are also used. Yagbongwura Nyantachi's title is commonly known as "Nyantachi *a'fari*." In the Tuluwewura's Kuntunkure appellation, we find in one stanza the use of the word "fa" for "sovereign."

European records also gives us more information about the Mande. The Manding nation is absolutely devoid of unity and one must undoubtedly go back far into history in order to find it with a government recognised by all the country. Each village lives separately under its own chief and, although these chiefs all belong to two or three illustrious families, yet in spite of their ties of relationship they have no solidarity of interest. This lack of cohesion between people of the same nation has already produced very bad effects in putting them at the mercy of the Tokolor. . . . Yet strangely enough, these profound divisions and the isolation of each group have not destroyed the ancient national

---

4 J. Spencer Trimingham, *A History of Islam in West Africa*, pp. 174–5. (Oxford University Press; 1965 reprint).

5 "J. le Maire (*Voyages* 1695) gives some information about the Wolof and their relation with Moorish clergy. A little before 1685 de la Courbe reports that the Moors profited from the discord reigning in the Wolof states to incite the people to kill the *barak* and expel the *damel* and the *bur-bar-Jolof* from their states. Afterwards Jolof rulers again gained the ascendancy. The *damel* Ditchiu-Maram, dispossessed chieftainess Yasin, mother of his predecessor, and she offered her self in marriage to a cleric, Ndyay Sal, on condition that he incited his disciples against the *damel*. In the encounter the *damel* was killed and succeeded by his brother under the patronage of Ndyay Sal. The assassination of the new *damel* by the cleric's disciples led to the intervention of the *bur* of Salum and the destruction of the Muslim party" (quoted by J. Spencer Trimingham in his *History of Islam in West Africa*, p. 176, note 1).

pride and the Mandings speak with emphasis of the Keyta and the Kamara from whom they descend.[6]

During the period of the great Wolof state many small chieftaincies had been formed among the southern Serer. A little before the first Portuguese arrived Mandinka, migrating from N'gabu (Portuguese Guinea) region, settled among them and took over the chieftaincies of Sin, Salum, Baol, Uli, Niani, and N'gabu, which were linked by various political ties with those of the Wolof. The ruling class of Mande origin (known as "gelowar" in Sin and Selum and "garmi" in Walo, Kajo, and Baol) are said to have been Muslims of a sort when they took over the Serer states, but they soon lost their Mande characteristics and became pagan. The most important Serer states were Sin situated on the right bank of the Salum river, and Salum adjoining Sin inland, whose authority at one time extended to the River Gambia. The tiny Serer states of N'Dukuman, Kungeul, Pakalla, Mandak, Rip, Legem and Niombato generally paid allegiance to either Sin or Salum.[7]

Greater initiative was shown by the Mande trading element who were definitely Muslim and spread Islam into upper Guinea and the Upper Ivory Coast. This region is peopled by Mandinka in the West (Beyla founded in 1763, Kankan c. 1690, Kurussa and Odienne region) and Senufo (Sienne or Sienamana) in the centre and east. Other Mandinka migrations came from the west, from the Upper Niger and upper Milo (Wasulonke, Futanke and Dyomane). These immigrants were pagans, but the trading classes among them were Muslims and Muslim Mande spread over the regions of Kankan and Beyla (in the east of Guinea) and in Odienne, Tuba, Man, Kong and Segela (upper Ivory Coast), Wa and Salaga (modern Ghana), and in Mossi country.[8]

6 Galliéni, *Voyage au Soudan Français (1870–1881)*, 1885, p. 338 (quoted by J. Spencer Trimingham, op. cit., p. 186).

7 Op. cit., p. 175.

8 Op. cit., pp. 186–7.

CHAPTER 1
The Mandingo Expedition to Bono Manso

At some time between 1550 and 1575 the great Askia Dawud of Songhay found that the supplies of gold from the southern country were getting smaller. The main reason was that Akan gold producers had begun selling some of their production to Portuguese and other European traders along the Seaboard.

Askia Dawud accordingly despatched a force of Mandinka armed cavalry to see what could be done. Dawud's armoured horsemen, the bulldozing tanks of these times, rode south from the neighbourhood of Jenne until they reached the Black Volta bend of modern Ghana.[9]

These horsemen were the ancestors of the present day Gonjas. The horse riders were armed with swords and iron spears. In war the horsemen acted as cavalry. The Gonjas discovered that cavalry could not operate in the dense forest where the Akan lived and smelted gold.

The Kuntunkure traditional drummer in some of the verses he recites gives us some information about the battles fought including those fought with the Akan.

In the verses entitled "Chari," the Mo-wura's (Manwura) appellation, we are informed that:

> It was at Dja and Kong towns that he [the Gonja leader Chari, or Saara] went and killed [defeated]
> Limu, the Dja and Kong towns hunter [warrior].
> They were two head hunters [war leaders]
> They bent and discharged [guns and arrows].
> This was before he [Chari Manwura] came to Manwule,
> Before he marched to Manwule Manso.
> It was at Long's town [Long-Kuro] that he went and killed Longoro [god] Bori Pasai.

9 Basil Davidson with F.K. Buah. *The Growth of African Civilisation: A History of West Africa 1000–1800* (Longman).

He [Bori Pasai] boasted much,
But could do nothing worthy.
This was before he came to Manwule,
Before he marched to Manwule Manso.
It was at Birim [town] that he went and killed,
The Djan Wiiri of Birim town,
[Birim was] a large forest [army]
But it was defeated at the river bank.
This was before he came to Manwule
Before he marched to Manwule Manso.
It was at Jape [Jape-Krom] that he went and killed
Kusugla of Jape;
This was before he came to Manwule,
Before he marched to Manwule Manso
"[The founder of] Manwule is a Hunter [Warrior]!"
"[The founder of] Manwule is a Ferryman."

Manwule was the first capital town established by the Gonjas on the northern bank of the Black Volta River.

The Mbontokurbi drummer also informs us in one of his verses:

The Dingo people [Man-Dingo adventurers] are arrayed against themselves.
On the battle field [territorial grounds] of the King of Kwakwau [Gao];
Some rode their horses on the reverse, facing backwards.
Remember the day of the battle of Sewfi;

In 1560–91, the Sultan Moulay Ahmed of Morocco, desirous of gaining control of the principal sources of West African gold, despatched a small but well-equipped expedition across the Sahara. The Askia Ishak of Songhay was crushingly defeated at Tondibi, the first battle in the Western Sudan in which firearms played an important part. Within a matter of months the Moors had established military control over the banks of the Niger from Gao to Jenne and the Songhay empire was in full dissolution. With this defeat of what one would term their home government, the Mandingo leaders who were sent out to Bono Manso may well have considered it the better part of valour not to return to their homeland but rather to set themselves up as independent rulers somewhere beyond the reach of the Moors.[10]

---

10 Because of this calamity caused to the Mandingoes by greed for gold, the Gonjas now abhor gold and do not want to possess it. It is generally claimed that gold has a bad omen and that if it is with a family the house will soon be in ruins. A nugget possessed by a Gonja family becomes an object of worship to which sacrifices are made periodically and it cannot be sold or used for an ornament.

When the Gonjas arrived in the Akan forest country they settled at Beawu (known in history books as Begho) and Ndziau. In the Banda area the tradition of the passage of the Gonjas is very much alive. To the Banda people the towns of Beawu (Begho) and Ndziau are also known as the Ponkowura krom—the village of the "Horse-Chief."

The Tachiman tradition as recorded by Meyerowitz[11] states that Nana Berampong Katakyira, whose reign is said to have lasted from 1564 to 1595 sacrificed himself by starvation at the time of the invasion by the Mande under Jakpa, "Ja-a kpa" is a title meaning "Conqueror with the Spears." In a later book,[12] she speaks of a Mande invasion of Bono Manso at the beginning of this reign which preceded Jakpa's conquest of Western Gonja. This date is consistent with that given in an Arabic manuscript for the reign of Lamba (Naba'a 1564/5–1593/4) who was the first King of the Gonjas in this part of Africa.

The Gonja Songhay leaders who headed the Gonja army to Bono Manso, in order of seniority were:

1. Lamba (Naba'a) who became the first king and whose reign began in about 1564/5;
2. Wam;
3. Lata or Lanta [popularly known as Dingoro Jakpa];
4. Lemu;
5. Jaffa;
6. Manfu;
7. Manwura [Chari]
8. Jakpa, popularly known as Ndewura Jakpa, who became the actual founder of the Gonja Empire.

Wam succeeded Lamba (Naba'a) as king when Lamba died. The Tachiman and Nkoranza people fought the Gonjas during the reign of Wam and succeeded in killing Wam. Lata or Lanta (Dingoro Jakpa) however drove the enemy away and left the area after a quarrel arose about the succession to the kingship and there was a plot to murder him.

Lata, as he is known by oral traditions, and Lanta as he is called in Arabic manuscripts, was also known as Nana Ekupo, that is, "grandfather warrior." Lanta was fighting on the battle field when the plot to kill him

---

The legend about gold is that it travels in the night and emits sparks of fire. Some gold pieces are said to be as long as serpents and that one could see them travelling at night with their long beams of light. The long line of warriors, with their firearms, who travel in a single formation on footpaths, possibly at night, in search of the sources of gold may be the serpents and fire meant. The long line of warriors are however referred to in the Kuntunkure drum verses as "Serpents."

11 Eva L.R. Meyerowitz, *Akan Traditions of Origin* (London, 1952).

12 Ibid., *The Akan of Ghana* (London, 1958).

was hatched. A message was sent to summon him from the battle field by the King, saying that his presence at a Council was urgently needed. Before his arrival, a deep pit was dug in the King's hall and the pit was covered with hides to conceal it. The Kuntunkure drummer knew about this plot but had no opportunity to inform Lata. Lata answered the King's summons with haste. He arrived when the King and the other leaders were seated in the hall awaiting his arrival.

As soon as he appeared at the door of the hall the King and almost all his colleagues pointed out to him the hides, which were placed over the pit, and invited him to go and sit there, saying that they were anxiously awaiting him as a very important decision had to be taken. Lata hesitated because he had never been received in that way before and it was not usual for him to sit on hides in the presence of the King. At that moment his brother-in-law, the Kuntunkure drummer, gave him the following message on the drum:

> Take care, be careful;
> A careful person does not fall in deep pits;
> Here sits a powerful animal [man]
> Wishing to deceive a Mo migrator
> To alight in the compound to be caught.
> A would be Mo Migrator does not deceive
> A fellow Mo Migrator
> There are deep pits,
> Covered with hides.

The Kuntunkure drummer referred to the place the Gonjas were then settled as Mo country and the King was styled Mo-wura, that is, King of Mo. Events proved that it was time Lata migrated from the area and the Kuntunkure drummer had decided to go with him.

On receiving the drum message Lata told the King that he felt like urinating and so he should be excused for a moment. He left the place and as soon as he reached his horse, which was still unsaddled, he rode on it and bolted away. The King and the other leaders could not understand Lata's action. They looked at each other and one of them pointed to the Kuntunkure drummer and said "this is the man who had warned him." He was right. After this incident, Lata composed a verse which has become the appellation of the Kuntunkure drummers. The title of the verse is "Lata Ngbanya inu m bul aso," meaning "Lata's Gonja must hear and fill their ears." They must understand the drum messages and their metaphorical language. The literal translation of the verse is:

> Lata's Gonjas must hear and fill their ears.
> He who hears and fills the ears,
> Is master of the deaf.
> Our country men do not suffer

The bullying of their chief.
If you dare say
"Chief, I bully you!"
The reserved army will ascend over those who are supposed to be the
vanguard.
There is deceit in the cheeks of the mate (Manwura)
But wisdom [on Lata's part] will have to act on its own.

After this incident Lata and Manwura never met. Lata regarded his
deserting Manwura as his having been exiled by him and we have the
Kuntunkure verse entitled "Chari Wam-mu," meaning "Chari, head of
the Wam retinue" expressing his feelings in these words:

Lata [said to] Limu,[13]
"If you can, make a farm [establish your own stake]
And eat from your farm." [make a living from your state]
I, [Lata] am washing the hands,
And they [my enemies] say I am usurping the King.
Will I, the exiled army,
Not turn him [Chari] into porridge water?
And fill my stomach with it and sit down?
If you object, or oppose, you should know how to act;
It is I, the cunning, who can fight a tournament.
It is he [Chari] who has the opportunity of being a sovereign
Who calls [elderly] princes by their names,
You [the elderly prince] know his name, and yet he commands you.

Lata Jakpa crossed the Black Volta River in his self-imposed exile and
settled at Kapuyase. He established a state between the White and the
Black Volta River which is known as the Dibir area. When Lata became
very old he created for himself the Burre Chieftainship and became
Burrewura in 1634/5. Burrewura became the most senior chief and Burre
the most senior office in the Gonja political system, senior to the
Yagbongwura, who is the effective head.

Lemu, the fourth leader, accompanied by Jaffa and Manfu the fifth
and sixth leaders took command of some of the men of the Gonjas
(Mande) army and fought the following countries, which lie northwest
of Bonduku, which they subdued: Palaga, Kong, Jimin, Awuasu,
Kongolu, Kwayini and Samata. Lemu was pacified with a house and
cattle when he marched on Gbona. Lemu died at Gbona.

Jaffa, the fifth leader, succeeded Lemu and came to Bole accompanied
by Manfu, the sixth leader. Manfu also died at Bole. Jaffa, now the only
surviving leader leading the group marched towards the east and con-

---

13 Limu was Manwura's brother.

quered the Kparba countries north of Salaga and the area of Kpanshogu, Kakpande and Jantong came under his jurisdiction. Jaffa might have found that Bolewura had already been given charge of the area when he arrived in Bole and it was necessary for him to establish his own state.

One of the reasons why Lata the third leader left Bono Manso and crossed the Black Volta River was that, on the death of Wam he, being the next in line of succession, by virtue of the order of seniority, was refused the Kingship and Manwura, the seventh leader and son of Lamba the first King, succeeded Wam. This might have been the reason why Lemu, Jaffa and Manfu also left Begho to establish their own states.

The tradition surrounding the town of Begho is that the inhabitants of Nsoko say that the town consisted of three groups, the Muslims (Karamoko), the Brongs (Abronfo) and the Blacksmiths (the Tonfo or Numu) although at Hani itself, the chief spoke of the Muslims, the Brongs and the Nafana. The town of Begho itself was said to have had two major sections, the Muslim part to the west of the small river of Masamo, and the pagan side to the east. The dispersal of its inhabitants was caused by a quarrel between members of these two groups, who then split up and occupied various villages not only in the country nearby but also farther afield.

Manwura (Chari Manwura) the seventh leader, who was now king, also crossed the Black Volta River at the head of the remaining Gonja Mande army and settled at a place called Manwule which became his capital. The Gonja capital was later removed to Gbipe (Buipe).

About this dispute over the kingship the Kuntunkure drummer tells us in the verse Kur Burre, i.e., "The challenging Burre [king]":

> The Kur Burre!
> On the battle field of fight for much [territory]
> I was to have been the Mo-wura [Mo-king]
> The claimant's [Chari] army fought
> Against the head of the Kurs [challengers].
> If he the [Kur Burre] catches the Mowura's army
> He will put them in fetters,
> And sit them on the arena.
>
> Here he [Kur Bure] is, here he is, just say!
> Don't allow him to say I've not said [to deny accusations].
> And then you cause casualties amongst the Oku men
> In order to be able to reign.
>
> The Kur Burre
> Gives life to lizards [people]
> And gives home to lizards. When the peoples home becomes ruins by destruction.
> If a leper [a light coloured man] bites you, you should also bite him.

Do not on account of his leprosy [light colour] allow him to walk about boasting.

CHAPTER 2
Extract from Arabic Manuscript

In an Arabic manuscript which was written by Imam Imoru, son of Imoru and Al-Haj Mahama, son of Mustapha and Mahama, son of Abdulahi the story of which ends in 1760, it is stated in the beginning of the work.

In the name of God the Compassionate, the Merciful, in remembrance of the people of old, and of the father of the mallam Mahama Labayiru, son of Ismaila who came with his son to the town of Ghofe (Gbipe or Buipe); he came to the Chief of Gonja whose name was Naba'a (Lamba); he came to the chief of Gonja who was at war in Kafiashi (Kapuyase).[14]

He was received with honour but on their way back to their town, God have mercy on his soul, he died at Sanfi and the news of his death was brought to his friend Naba'a (Lamba—the first Gonja King).

And they said, "Your friend, the Mallam Ismaila, is dead;" so the Chief (at Kapuyase) sent much money to his brother at Gofe to offer prayers and to give alms. They offered prayers and the people of the country of the Blacks saw this and did likewise, each one making prayers and giving alms as he was able.

Then they took his son, who was also a mallam, Mohamed Labayiru, and he went in amity to the Chief, his father's friend. But he did not find him alive, instead he found his son, the Manwura, sitting in the place of the chief Naba'a. He found him at Kolo, and the day, a Friday, he found him fighting fiercely. The midday sun was strong and they were fighting in the sun; but the Mallam saw a large and shady tree close to the scene of battle.

So the Mallam said to the chief of Gonja "Let us go under the shade of the tree." The chief of Gonja replied "How can we get a chance to go and sit under the tree; it is so close to the fight that we cannot rest there."

---

14 The visit was to two different chiefs, one at Gbipe and the other at Kapuyase.

The Mallam replied "If God so wills it, we will drive off the unbelievers and then sit at the foot of the tree."

Then the Mallam went in front and the chiefs of the Gonja followed until they came to the foot of the tree. In his hand the Mallam carried a staff, the handle of which was covered with leather. He planted it in the grounds, he struck the ground and planted the staff in the earth between the contestants. So when he did this and the enemy saw they fled. By the power of God did he do this.

Then the Gonjas opened the gates of Kolo and entered the town and when the Chief of Gonja saw what the Mallam had done, he was astonished and said "Behold, the religion of these people surpasses our own."

So the Gonjas became envious and wished to adopt Islam. So the Chief became a Moslem, together with his brother called Amoah, with Limu and with Jafa and Mafa, the twins who were the sons of a Moslem. His brothers Amoah and Limu died; at that time Mafa and Jafa, the paternal nephews of the Chief the Manwura were children. When they grew up they followed in the faith of their uncle the Manwura, Chief of Gonja.

When the Gonjas repented (were converted) the Mallam gave them new names. Now the Manwura's name was Sa'ara, and the Mallam gave him the name of Imoru Kura. The name of Amoa was also Imoru; and Limu was called Imoru Saidu; Jafa, Al Hassan; and Mafa, Al Hussein.[15] They all repented (were converted) on the same day.

Naba'a ruled for thirty years before he died, and his successor ruled for nineteen years. He built the mosque at Ghofe (Buipe). Amoah was also Al Haji, because he gave money to one to go and represent him on the pilgrimage. The man went and prayed there and returned to Ghofe and so Amoah became Chief and ruled for twenty-one years. But the Mallams disputed this and say he ruled for two years more.

Now behold Lanta, who is Jakpa, entered into Bura and he became the Burre-Wura.[16] When he was chief he became very powerful; among all those who had gone before him, not one would equal him as a ruler. Everything concerning his kingdom he took into his own hands; he divided the country of Gonja and gave it to his brothers. When he became chief there was no one who dared dispute with him, and the power has remained in the hands of the brothers right down to the present day. When he died in the year of the Hegira 1093, the Mallams say, he had

---

15 Manwura, Amoah, Limu, Jafa and Mafa were of one family or lineage. It does not appear from the record that Lata (Lanta) and his people were also converted at the same time.

16 It is a significant point to note that when Amoah Imoru Saidu Al Haji in the Manwura lineage died in 1634/5 Lanta (Lata Dii Ngoro Jakpa) became Burrewura. The Kingship was therefore taken away from the Manwura lineage by the Lata Ngbanya.

ruled for forty-two years. He was very old and when he was ready to take the Chieftainship of Bura (Burre) he handed over his kingdom to his son, who was called So'ara after his grandfather but was also called So'ara Sulemanu.[17]

He was the son of Lanta, and he had ruled only for six years when his father of Bura died. After this he ruled for sixteen years. His rule lasted for twenty-two years. During his reign he conquered many lands and made war on many towns, and because there was continual war he was deposed (killed in the Ashanti war). The Mallams say that when he was deposed (defeated) it was in the year of Hegira 1109.

17 Some traditional historians also refer to the Manwura as Bur (Burre) Manwura. So'ara is Chari in the Kuntunkure drum verses.

CHAPTER 3
Chari Manwura (1595/6 [or 1593/4] to 1614/5 [or 1612/3])

As can be seen from the extract quoted above the Gonjas were pagan Mandingos and were converted to Islam by Mallam Mohamed Labayiru, who came to be known as Fati Morukpe, after their victory over the Kolo (Kawlaw) army. The Gonjas were partially converted and have remained nominal Muslims to this day, because the majority of them still worship idols, and it is a taboo up to this present day, in eastern Gonja at least where the Gonjas are more conservative, for a Gonja Chief to enter a Mosque to pray. The Gonjas were partially converted to Islam because they were impressed by the miraculous routing of the enemy at Kawlaw and wanted to keep the Muslims to make prayers unto Allah for them so that they could continue to win victory in all their wars. This would enable them to establish their own Kingdom and thereby increase their fortunes by accumulating more worth.

After their conversion Chari Manwura asked Mallam Mohammed Labayiru (Fati Morukpe) to take service with him and offer prayers for him unto Allah so as to divert mishaps and evils which might tend to bar his advance and promised to reward him if he were successful in his adventure. An agreement was made at the camp, which was sealed by an oath taken on the Quran, binding both parties to keep the agreement. The agreement was:

   i. That Fati Morukpe should go with the Ngbanya (Gonja) army and implore God for its success;

   ii. That the articles of reward comprising;

   One hundred slaves (men and women)
   One hundred cattle,
   One hundred horses,
   One hundred donkeys,
   One hundred sheep,
   One hundred goats,
   One hundred gowns,

One hundred pairs of trousers, and
One hundred of everything that would be found in the new
Kingdom when founded, should be paid to Fati Morukpe when
he, Chari Manwura, had established himself and settled as
Emperor over the countries that would fall to him and

iii. That if either or both Chari Manwura and Fati Morukpe should die
before the acquisition of the hoped for kingdom, the oath should be
honourably kept by the descendants of both parties and the promises
fulfilled by the heirs and successors of Chari Manwura, and that the
reward be paid to the descendants of Fati Morukpe, who came to be
known by the Gonjas as the Sakpare Mallams (Sakpare Nsua).[18]

After entering into this Agreement with Chari Manwura, the King of
Gonja, Fati Morukpe again entered into a similar agreement with Lata
(Lanta) Dii Ngoro Jakpa. The entering into agreements with both leaders
strongly suggests that Chari Manwura and Lata Dii Ngoro Jakpa were
independent sovereigns and had become allies.

Oral tradition claims that Manwura travelled to this country in an
iron boat whilst Lata Jakpa travelled with his cavalry. Manwura, it is
said, died in his iron-boat which sank at Lurnchira where the White and
the Black Volta Rivers meet. This was where Lata Jakpa established his
state, with his seat at Kapuyase. It is difficult to see how Manwura
travelled in a boat[19] to Bono Manso, and then to Gbipe, because there
is no river coming from Jenne directly to Gbipe where he finally settled.
If the Manwura actually used an "iron boat" on the Black Volta River
then it might have been carried across country part of the way.

In the Kuntunkure drum verses there are references to a "sailing-
bridge" and a "firing-bridge" which means a naval boat and whereas the
Yagbonwura, the descendant of Lata, has a bow and quiver for his
insignia the Gbipewura the descendant of Manwura, has a boat.

We have in the drum verses the following stanzas:

Departure from the firing-bridge;
Departure from the sailing-bridge;
[stanzas found in the verse Jaga which is the Bolewura's appellation].
On the day of battle in [Sonni] Ali's place [kingdom]
It was there that he constructed a river,
And by-passed the bridge [naval fleet].

---

18 The Sakpare Mallams have been distributed and attached to courts of the Paramount
and Divisional Chiefs. They are the Gonja Chiefs hereditary Imams and they have a
prescribed role in the enrobement of Chiefs and in the performance of many customary
functions.

19 The use of a boat may possibly be by Manwura's predecessors when they travelled
from Mande to the Songhay Empire on the River Niger.

[Stanzas found in the verse Danga which is the
Damongowura's appellation.]

In the verse entitled "Chari," which is the Mo-wura's (Man-wura)
appellation, the following stanzas are found:

The springer of surprises,
Chari is the one who does it;
He sits in the river,
And musters animals [men] together.
He is a small town [a small army]
But it is a big town [large armies] that he fights.
At Silima he crossed water [sailed] and captured a chief.
At Bangpe he sailed and captured a chief.
[There was also with him]
The head of the Sousou,
Who brought the drummers.
The head of the Saints who brought confiscators,
And they came to display, encircling [with horses].
"[The founder of] Manwule is a Hunter [warrior]"
"[The founder of] Manwule is a Ferryman."

With all these references to the boat man and naval fleet, which no
doubt refers to the Gonjas former home, one could conclude that
Manwura might have been an officer of the Songhay fleet before his
departure to this country. The claim that the Manwura's iron boat sank
at Lurnchira is no doubt proverbial. What is meant is that he lost his
authority and control over the person, Lata Jakpa, who established a state
in that area. As far as the people of that state were concerned, he was to
them dead and not to be taken account of.

This further confirms that Manwura and Lata Dii Ngoro Jakpa were
leaders of two different or separate groups of people. On ceremonial
occasions it is the duty of the Sakpare Mallams to say prayers before the
Paramount or Divisional Chief and to ask for God's blessing for the Chief
and his predecessors who must all be mentioned by their names. The
prayer of blessings starts with Manwura. The prayer is as follows in
Kpembe:

Manwura, may God bless him; may God forgive him his sins.
Iwur-Kakar (The Junior/Vice Chief) may God bless him; may
God forgive him his sins. Ndewura Jakpa, may God bless him,
may God forgive him his sins. Bur-Kpembewura, may God bless
him, may God forgive him his sins.

Iwur-Kakar (the Vice Chief) is no other than Lata Jakpa who comes
before his son Ndewura Jakpa, and Bur Kpembewura is Kpembewura

Mahama Labayiru who succeeded Abbas and was the last absolute monarch who, as Yagbongwura, had his residence at Gbipe. In the verse entitled "Akpa-wura" (the Spear man), which is Kapuyasewura's (Chief of Kapuyase) appellation, the poet says:

> The Prince of Say,[20] the place of the weak army.
> Mightiness calms down,
> As a hawk calms down.
> He who preceded the Gonjas to burn down towns [Manwura],
> If you come this way again,
> You branch to see;
> The cheeky fox [Jakpa]
> He captured and ate [vanquished] him.
> The Kur (challenging) group which annexes other groups;
> He (Sulemana) who was to fall unknowingly;
> He was a bubble (only) a bubble;
> He was a victim of the Jakpa family!
>
> Here are his comrades,
> Sitting on top of walls [as sovereigns]
> They carry him [in a palanquin] by day,
> And he may come to walk by night [going into exile].
> Will that night not come?

The verse might have been composed after the defeat of Sulemana and Kapuyase was Lata Jakpa's headquarters. The year 1614/5 (or 1612/3) therefore marked the beginning of the founding of modern Gonja. The Mbontokurbi drummer has this to say about the three founding Fathers in the verse entitled "Dii Ngoro Jakpa":

> Manwura, Fati Morukpe, Dii Ngoro Jakpa [the three allies]
> The quiver that fills the house [builds the state].
> The Dagombas want to fight
> The Kob that drives away animals.
> The Dingo [Man-Dingo] adventurers are arrayed against themselves,
> On the territorial ground of the King of Kawkaw [Gao]
> Some rode their horses on the reverse [facing the tail of the horse].
> Remember:
> The day of the battle with Manwu [Manwura]
> The day of the battle of Sewfi.[21]

---

20 Say is a town on the River Niger south of Gao in the former Kawkwa state under the Askiya Dynasty.

21 It is probable that Manwura did not die a natural death but died in a struggle. His grave is said to be at the foot of a hill called Longbonbe near Mpaha in the Dibir area.

The Kuntunkure drum verses are in metaphorical language and one has to be instructed very well to be able to understand them. Names of animals and birds, such as hyena, cow, fowl, cock, guinea-fowl, etc. have been used in some of the verses instead of using the real names or titles of the persons referred to.

CHAPTER 4
Ndewura Jakpa (1675–97)

From the time of the taking of the oath on the Qur'an open hostilities between Chari Manwura and Lata Dii Ngoro Jakpa ceased. In 1675/6 Lata Dii Ngoro Jakpa abdicated and handed over the sovereignty to his son who was given the title of "Ndewura Jakpa." Lata Dii Ngoro Jakpa became Burrewura[22] in 1634/5 and therefore sovereign of the Lata Ngbanya (Gonjas) for 41 years when he died in 1681/2. It was Ndewura Jakpa who expanded the Gonja Empire by conquest. All the land he conquered was Dagomba territory.

Limu, Manwura's brother who came after Amoah was still alive at the time Lata Jakpa(Burrewura) handed over his sovereignty to his son Ndewura Jakpa. Limu had expected that he would have succeeded Lata Jakpa.

Ndewura Jakpa began his conquests by first moving west from the Dibir country where his father founded his state. He marched towards Gbipe, Manwura's capital which town he by-passed, and marched through Sakpa into western Gonja (the Bole Division). There was now open hostility between the Lata Ngbanya and the Manwura's group, and one Sulemana became an active leader of the Manwura's people. Limu might have been too old at that time to be able to give effective leadership.

At Sakpa the elders of Bel (Bole), Mandari and Gbenfu met Ndewura Jakpa and surrendered to him. The town of Bel was renamed Bole meaning "Submission" in Gonja. After he had settled affairs in Bole and appointed a chief (the Bolewura) for the area Ndewura marched north.

---

22 The town of Burre was almost embedded in Mandingo country. In the Maghreb and in Europe the gold trade was particularly associated with the Mandingos whose wealth was proverbial. "There are no countries in the world richer in gold and silver than the Kingdoms of Mandinga" wrote Purchase (E.W. Bovill, *The Golden Trade of the Moors* (London: Oxford University Press, 1963), p. 194. Gold logs, instead of lighted logs, were said to be placed before the Burrewura when he complained that he was feeling cold.

He met with strong resistance at the town of Gbongori. This was a Dagomba town and the Dagombas called it Bunduraya. Ndewura Jakpa fought the town for two months before it fell. The fetish priest of the town rode on a donkey and he was on the top of the flat roof houses almost all the time.

After the defeat of the town Ndewura Jakpa entered it and after resting for some time he appointed Jafow Sonni as the Chieftainess of the town. The town was renamed "Mankuma" that is, "Man ko ma" meaning "a state that fights me." At this particular moment news was reaching Ndewura Jakpa about the activities of Limumu and Sulemana Chari and the Gbipe people. His comments were composed into a Kuntunkure verse entitled "Lajipo ba imboe" (the soothsayer who binds [annexes] animals [people]), and the verse became the appellation of Mankuma town. The translation of the verse is as follows:

> Limu and the great woman,
> That is Shari [Chari Sulemana].
> You have already backbited me,
> And I have already heard [what you said]
> That was why I came away
> With a swollen cheek [annoyed].
> [Your complaint was]
> "Mother, the Deys [Lata Jakpa and Ndewura Jakpa] have exchanged places in order to be able to reign. In order to be able to reign, they have differentiated me with small homes."
> Limu came with the woman who has befriended the soothsayers.
> He who is first [to offend] teaches another [to retaliate].
> He who comes first [as an adventurer]
> Is the gatherer [sovereign].

Another Kuntunkure verse was also composed for the town of Manwule which might have been in existence during the time Ndewura Jakpa conquered Mankuma. The verse is entitled "Manwule Bey so," meaning "The Manwule Bey trapper," the literal translation of which is:

> The Manwule Bey trapper [versus]
> The Bey trapper, Lanta the Kur head
> [Head of the challengers]
> A discipliner of animals [people].
> Whenever he [the Manwule Bey] lies down,
> The vultures [enemies] scratch.
> His executioner is Lata Limu, to strike whilst rage is ineffective.
> The enraged striker is the Manwule Bey trapper.
> The junior Bey trapper [Ndewura Jakpa] has marked
> The red-fighter-ant [Sulemana]
> It is God who gives the Burre army drink [Sovereignty].

Lata Jakpa was still then alive. We will see him mentioned in the Dbiriwura's message to Ndewura Jakpa when he was further north asking him to return south to meet the enemy who was manouvering.

THE CREATION OF THE YAGBONG CHIEFSHIP— K'YAGBONGWURA

Whilst in the north country Ndewura Jakpa received a message from his nephew, the Dibirwura asking him to return south as Sulemana whom he styled the "wild hyena" had attacked him. Sulemana was then Chefijiwura—Chief of the people from Zafizi. The Mos who were under Manwura's control migrated from Zafizi in the Issala country in the north and settled south of the Black Volta River. It was probably for this reason that Sulemana was styled the Chief of Chefiji (Chefijiwura).

The Dibirwura's message to Ndewura was composed into a verse and that has become the Dibirwura's Kuntunkure appellation. It is entitled "Kul Wan De" (Hawk, the Dagomba Dey), and it is:

> Hawk, Dagomba Dey!
> Mo [army] manoeuvres;
> Come down south
> Come and narrate and slaughter.
> Prince!
> The man who fights other armies,
> And other forces fight his animals [people].
> The infirm!
> Dey Say Lanta!
> The wild hyena [Sulemana] deceived himself.
> He [Dibirwura] struck the Hyena
> And made it stiff, thereby fettering him
> For the Hawk, the Dagomba Dey.
> His [Dibirwura's] uncle is the Black-smith [Ndewura Jakpa]
> Who fetters.
> There he [Dibirwura] pinned them down,
> Nibbling at the Hyena's [Sulemana] little armies.
> He [Ndewura Jakpa] faces the Hyena!
> He also faces [the armies of] Dagomba land!
> Complicated matters.
> Matters are pouring in.
> To be in such trouble was not foreseen.
> The stirring army,
> Kill and take refuge in the Lii forest;
> The Dagomba Dey [Ndewura Jakpa] is not to blame.

Ndewura Jakpa came to Nyanga were he camped. It was here that the fox was to strike. He gave the Senyonwura the "large army"—with which to attack Sulemana Chefijiwura who was moving north, with these instructions, which have become the Senyonwura's Kuntunkure appellation:

> Receive the Chieftaincy of the Junior fox,—*So nyang bi wura*[23]
> And bid for the prince [Chefijiwura].
> He [Ndewura Jakpa] knows [what is happening]
> Yet he inquires.
> On the battle field of mouth drumming [narration].
> There he [Ndewura Jakpa] killed an executioner [decided the fate of an enemy],
> An installed an executioner [his vanquisher].
> If the Executioner [Sulemana] is unable [defeated],
> He will learn a lesson;
> If the bidder of defiance to the prince [Senyonwura]
> Does not return,
> He will learn a lesson;
> It is because the bidder for the prince
> Had understood his instructions well
> That he ably answered.

Senyonwura Lannyo met Sulemana Chefijiwura at a place which came to be called Chefiji and defeated his enemy. Sulemana retreated and was chased up to Fimbu where the Senyonwura stopped and returned to report his victory. All the area from Senyon to Fimbu, including Kabalma and Dakrupe became the Senyonwura's area of jurisdiction. Senyonwura became the first Yagbonwura and was at the same time the Seyonwura; he held doubled leadership.

The Kuntunkurewura informs us in the verse entitled "Chefijiwura" about Sulemana and the cause of the battle as follows:

> The Chefijiwura versus the Hawk of Mande!
> The embers[24] burned,
> Fighting their [separate] ways coming,
> Then the mate rekindled it.
> The mate deceived me, saying
> "Let me come with you,
> So that we conquer together!"
> Not knowing he was only full of deceit.
> "Exiled-army [Lata Jakpa], knowing how to narrate [compose verses]
> Is no art of hunting [fighting].
> If you'll only kneel here,

---

23 "*So*" in Gonja means "receive, help, deputize, substitute," as in the following sentences: "*So kake*"—receive a gift; "*So ma esulc*"—help me with my load; "*So m ba a ya son yo*"— go as my representative or substitute. "*So nyang*"—deputize for the fox (Jakpa).

24 The first Gonja leaders—Lamba and Lata Jakpa.

And kneel there,
Blood will not dry.
He who came first [Lamba]
Was the one who complicated matters.
Mate,
Knowing how to narrate,
Is no fault of mine."

Sulemana Chefijiwura was supposed to have said, when he decided to go into exile after his defeat, as is recited in the Kutunkure verse entitled "Kanan kin foi," meaning "If a clan rejects you,"

Our comrades have taken the opportunity
Of our not being many,
To regard us as people of another clan.
If a clan rejects you,
You go to join another clan;
Another different clan
Will not reject an ally.

From Nyanga Ndewura Jakpa went to Damongo. The town was known as Jingbaripe. He knew that the enemy Sulemana had suffered a crushing defeat and had gone into exile, heading for Ashanti.

It was at this time that Ndewura Jakpa's Kuntunkure appellation was composed. That appellation entitled "Jini akpa" ("Jakpa," for short) that is, "Conqueror with the Spears" has become the Yagbonwura's appellation:

Conqueror with the Spear!
The settler at Mo-nu [the Mo boundary]
Has finished his reign,
And only Jakpa is left
The *Kibir mpa*—the narrator of battles—has handed over to him [Jakpa]
And he sits and narrates them with pomp and dignity.
He [Jakpa] is now the Chief of Silima.
Victor in battles and wars.
He is now Chief of Mantam.[25]
Victor in battles and wars.

Patience, patience, the tortuous roving slave
Jakpa decides to march south;
He decides to march on the town of the
Former conquerors, the vanquished rebukers.
It was a retaliation that he besieged them, and opened for them a gate

---

25 Chieftainess belonging to the Gbipe princes.

Through which to scatter [and go into exile].
The people of Mantam built fortresses,
And said they would fight Jakpa;
The strong animal (man) stepped with a large army and crushed them.
The people of Silima built a fortress
And said they would fight Jakpa;
The strong animal stepped with a large army,
And crushed them.
The Kong-shi[26] [sovereigns] built fortresses,
And said they would fight Jakpa,
The strong animal stepped with a large army,
And crushed them.
The Eagle!
The man who eats [reigns] and other birds [men] sit by:
The spark of fire
That falls upon the bush
And set the bush blazing.
The great force with which he disciplines the Ngbanya [Gonjas]
Is the same that he uses in controlling the Nyamase [autochthonous inhabitants].

With *aburabi* [Cotton thread] he held the [Muslims]
[He is as strong as] Ntim [Gyakari] who binds the *Mbong* [Ashantis];[27]
With *echuniifa* [fibre of the husks of dawadawa fruits] he held the Ndare [Dagartis].
With *efulpuntung* [fibre of local rope] he held the Dagombas.
With *gibichin* [grass used for basket weaving]
He held the Ngurinshi [Grunshis].

Jakpa! The layer in ruins of large towns,
Whilst small towns stand and shiver.
An old hyena!
He exhumes the dead bodies.

From Damongo Ndewura Jakpa headed in the direction of Kusawgu. He camped at "Nyan-wur-pe" and directed operations against the Dagombas in the Kusawgu area. After the defeat of the Dagombas he put his youngest son in charge of the area and came to Salaga marching through Kafaba.

---

26 "Shi" is a title for sovereign in the Songhay Empire as, Si Madogo, who started the conquest of the dependencies to Mali in 1463. Si Dandi, who pillaged Mima in 1400, and Si Ali the great, who was the eighteenth Si and who founded the Songhay Empire.

27 At the time of the Gonja invasion the Ashantis were under Denkyira Kings. Ntim Gyakari reigned from 1695 to 1699 and it was during his reign that the Ashantis defeated the Denkyiras. Ndewura Jakpa was defeated by the Ashantis in 1697, two years before the defeat of Denkyira.

Ndewura Jakpa never went to Ashanti. Sulemana styled himself as Jakpa, King of Yagbong, when he went into exile and the people of all the places he went through refer to him as Jakpa. This has confused many historians. It was Sulemana who passed through Prang; when people refer to Jakpa having passed that way it is Sulemana who is meant. Passing near a village Sulemana's attention was drawn to it and he remarked "ma kpalang bumu so," that is to say "take no notice of them." From that time the place came to be known as Kpalang a name by which the Brongs of Prang know it.

According to Pranghene Nana Kofi Dante and the Queenmother Yaa Nsia and their elders Prang used to be called Gyanewu (Gyane's Home). They said that the name "Kpalang" was given to the town during Ndawura Jakpa's time. When Jakpa who wanted to fight them missed the town and his attention was drawn to this fact, Jakpa said "Then better leave off fighting it," hence "Kpalang" (a Gonja word).[28]

According to them the first Chief of Prang was Nnyinawu Danga. The second chief was Komwe; the third chief was Ware Koku. The fourth Chief was Enwuku and the fifth Chief was Kpagya during whose time Jakpa passed near the town. The people of Prang fought on the side of Bono Techiman against Ashanti for seven years about 1730–40 according to Nana Kofi Dante. However, Sulemana Jakpa's exile would have been after 1675/6, six years after which Ndewura Jakpa's father, Lata Jakpa handed his power to Ndewura Jakpa but about a decade before 1697 when Ndewura Jakpa died.

After the conquest of the Kusawgu area Ndewura Jakpa met with no further resistance. The country of Salaga was occupied by the Nanumbas and Konkombas but the area was deserted when the people heard about Ndewura Jakpa's advance. Ndewura stayed in Kpembe for some time and after appointing a Chief for the area he continued his eastward march passing through the Alfai (Kpanda) area. The place was also deserted. He planted the Nawuras he brought with him in the place and appointed the Kanakulaiwura as the Chief of the area.

Having settled the affairs of the Alfai area Ndewura Jakpa went on to Sensane-Mango. Here he settled the Owin and Nzima people he took with him as captives, mercenaries and refugees in the wars with the Akans. These people are the Chakosis of the present day and they are joking mates of the Gonjas.

Ndewura Jakpa went up to Kagbaful in the Busari country. It was here that his followers showed signs of war weariness. The Kobs, as the Gonjas described themselves, were fed up. In Gonja the expression is "'k gba afol" and from this expression the name of the town Kagbafol was derived. Some people say that at this place the bridle rope "K'gbang fol"

28 ADM. 58/5/8; Ghana National Archives, Accra.

of Ndewura Jakpa's horse was broken when he was ascending a hill and that was the reason why the town was called K'gbafol. Of course, Ndewura Jakpa was styled the horse (gbanga) and it was in this place that he lost control over his people. The bridle could no longer be used effectively and so he could therefore not ascend on the hill of sovereignty in the Zugu country. It may be for this reason that the Kuntunkure appellation composed for the Kpembewura, was entitled "Bungang ebulbpo," meaning "Respect the Subject":

> Respect the subject
> And the subject will raid [for booty] to eat
> And give a share to the prince to eat.
> It is too many worries that prevent
> A prince from receiving gifts from the subject.
> It is a respectful chief
> Who wins the allegiance of people of different tribes.

Ndewura Jakpa returned to Kpembe where he built a palace and decided to make the place his permanent home.It is an admitted fact that Ndewura Jakpa went as far as the Zugu boundary where his people mutinied. By that time his army was made up of mercenaries and refugees of many different tribes, who he recruited as he made his conquests and advances. The mutiny stopped his advance further eastward and he had to return to Kpembe where he finally settled to administer his Kingdom. The ruins of Ndewura Jakpa's palace called K'wurwu to are still standing in Kpembe. It is the only known residence of Ndewura Jakpa in Gonja and it is said that honey was used in mixing the mortar for its construction.

The Mbontokurbi drummer in the verse entitled "Kali"[29] (an escape) informs us of this mutiny in the following words:

> Kali [the exile] comes [home] bringing life [no more fighting].
> Kali strikes spiritlessly.
>
> They [the mutineers] gathered sticks and beat Kali,
> "I have come" [said Kali] "oh room comrades [country men]
> Migrating exiles do not rule"
> (that is, refugees don't have subjects owing allegiance to them]
> The Exile,
> The overthrown San [Saint] is coming.
> Kali destroys fowl coops [small towns] and sleeps soundly.
> Kali is a gatherer of homes [peace maker].
> Mutiny confronted him at the Zugu boundary,

---

29 "Lii" in Gonja means "run." "I lii ga" means "he ran fast."

They [the mutineers] resisted the water [sovereign] and
Caught the serpents [his fighting men]
Children cry, blaming Kali [for their woe]
And women cry blaming Kali,
And he said, "If it is on my account, life would be spared;
I am [now like the] Kali Chari [the Vanquished Chari]"
Kali,
They [the mutineers] are in conflict
And he sits [watching].

In 1697 Ndewura Jakpa heard of an Ashanti invasion. There was no time for him to call for reinforcement from all the Divisions of Gonja as distances were far. Ndewura Jakpa met the Ashanti army at Talkpa, crossing the Volta River near Kafaba. The people in Kpembe who were war weary, were reluctant to fight and they tried to persuade Ndewura Jakpa not to leave Kpembe, and told him that a serpent that lived in the river at Yeji vomited poison and if the horses drank the water from the river they would die. He was not to be persuaded. "Tar kpa" means "where one stops" and it was at Tarkpa that the battle with the Ashantis took place. Ndewura Jakpa was mortally wounded. He was carried away from the battle field and he breathed his last at Shirminchu.[30] There was panic ("iburmu") among the Gonjas.

It was decided that Ndewura Jakpa's body should be buried at Nyanga but it got putrid when it arrived at Gbipe so it was buried there. Ndewura Jakpa's horse was led to Gbipe unsaddled and unridden, and up to the present day, the manner of announcing the death of the Paramount Chief of Gonja is to send his unsaddled horse, his staff and saddles to the Gbipewura (Chief of Gbipe).

The exiled Sulemana was installed at Gbipe as the sovereign of Gonja under the title "Jakpa." During the period of his reign historians were silent about him and there appeared to be an interregnum between 1697–1709, a period of twelve years.

This was because of his (Sulemana) perfidious action inviting the aid of the Ashanti to further his claims to the Gonja Paramountcy and the suffering brought to the whole of the Gonja people when the Gonja Kingdom became a vassal state of Ashanti and he the King of Ashanti's protégé—a Kabong-Jelli (Ashanti slave).[31]

---

30 "*Shir ma nchu*" is a challenge; it means "Meet me, water" "Water" is a metaphor for "sovereign" which has been frequently used in the Kuntunkure drum verses.

31 "Tradition, as the collective memory of a social group, is assured some form of continuity by its relationship to kingship and aristocracy. Noble families maintained professional archivists. In the Western cycle these are caste groups, called dyeli by Mande. Their function was to chant the genealogy, praise the noble deeds, and extol the exploits of the privileged. They transmitted to pupils of their own family the

Secondly, the Lata Ngbanya, Ndewura Jakpa's people, tried to succeed him but each of the successors lived for a very short period. This was because there was fighting between the Lata Ngbanya and Sulemana Jakpa, who was aided by the Ashantis, each side wanting to retain the Paramountcy. It was therefore difficult for historians to say who was the *de jure* king.

The poet tells us of the last moments of Ndewura Jakpa in the Kuntunkure verse entitled "Bowlong" (the red fighter ant) in these words:

"Red fighter-ant" [light coloured fighter];
A bad [son] in-law has complained against you [Ndewura Jakpa].
"Red fighter-ant" [the Exile Jakpa],
Make your complaint,
You receive certain reports,
And receive adverse reports,
The orphan's [Sulemana] in-law [the Ashanti King]
It is still fair with you.
"I sit on my wall [sovereignty]
I am from my wall descending.
May God let my mother-in-law
Die, and leave my father-in-law
When an orphan complains against a wife,
He often forgets the mothers
With every little matter,
She goes to the house of the mother.
And makes yarn of it.
On the battle field of the Solomon ants [inoffensive people]
There he [the mother-in-law] refused the migrator to forge.
If you kill the migrator [Ndewura Jakpa]
Who will forge for you your spears?
Bowlong [the red-fighter-ant] had shot and hit you [Ndewura Jakpa]
He [the enemy] has shot him in the waist;
Bad thoughts [of death] still hang round his [Ndewura Jakpa] neck."

---

accumulated traditions of the lineage or clan to which they were attached. They were always spared in war and not reduced to slavery and thus often came to devote their talents to new masters" (J. Spencer Trimingham, *A History of Islam in West Africa*, p. 3). Although the Gonjas were made to pay yearly tribute of slaves called *ayibodia* to the Ashanti King, as a result of Gonja becoming a vassal state of Ashanti, the Gonjas were not themselves accepted as slaves, and it was an offence to take a Gonja into Ashanti as a slave. The Gonjas had to raid the acephalous tribes of the north (the Grunshi, Sisala and Frafra) to provide Ashanti with the *ayibodia* (annual tribute of slaves). This was all because of Sulemana's association with Ashantis.

Ndewura Jakpa reigned for twenty-two years from the time of his Regency when his father Lata Jakpa (Burrewura) handed to him his sovereignty in 1675/6 to the time of his death in 1697.

CHAPTER 5
Sulemana Jakpa (1697–1709)

When in exile Sulemana[32] styled himself (Jakpa) the King of Yagbong and his settlement in Atebubu was a province under the chief of Mampong. Carl Christian Reindorf in his book The History of the Gold Coast and Ashanti (p. 83; 2d edn.) described this small Gonja settlement and states:

> As already mentioned, Opoku Ware during the whole of his reign was actively engaged in completing and strengthening the conquests of his predecessors in the north and north-east countries. The Nta country then governed by the King of Yebo (Yabong), a nominal province of Mampong, Owusu Sakyere of Mampong, who had charge of the province, sent messengers there to levy men for sacrifice to his late father; but the King of Yebo refused to permit it. Owusu Sekyere appealed to the King Opoku and war was declared against the Ntas. Opoku, as usual, seized his opportunity, marched his army there and subdued the whole country.

Sulemana married an Ashanti woman and some of the children he had with her were, Asantewa, Kofi Gyedu and Ko Agyapo. This is why the Ashanti King is described in the Kuntunkure verse Bowlong quoted above as the orphan's (Sulemana) "mother-in-law."

The name "Nta" was given to the Gonjas by the Ashantis possibly because of the bow (and arrows) with which Ndewura Jakpa was associated. The bow in Gonja is called "K'ta." Another reason may be that there were twin (two) Kings of Gonja at the time forming a condominium. First

---

32 Before the start of the Gonja Hunter's dance called *Kpana* the singers open the dance with the song Sulemani (Sulemana) Salamalaikum. The *alobi* dance performed by women also starts with the song *"Sulemani Kpatakpari brese, m sin na mang mu so,"* meaning "Sulemani the trapper has fallen, let us raise him up." At Larabanga the *taware* song also has something to say about Sulemani (see Appendix I).

Lanta,[33] Dii Ngoro Jakpa (Bur'wura) and Manwura; and secondly, Ndewura Jakpa and Sulemana Kabong Jakpa, who was in exile in Atebubu and who returned after Ndewura Jakpa's death to usurp the paramountcy. The name Nta or Ntafo has now been extended to cover all the peoples of the Northern and Upper Regions of Ghana. The territory controlled by Manwura was referred to, by the Akan people as Nta-fufuo Manso—the white Nta/twin state. According to the Gonja oral tradition, Manwura was white, i.e., light coloured and hairy.

When Sulemana Jakpa died he was buried in the mosque at Gbipe which was built by his predecessors. His Brong subjects carried bamboo sticks annually, bare-headed, for its repair. This Jakpa's grave is worshipped and it is the Gbipewura who offers the sacrifices. The Gbipewura is in charge of the sacred grave. I am convinced that it was Sulemana Jakpa and not Ndewura Jakpa who was buried in the Gbipe mosque because it is a taboo to build a mosque in Kpembe where Ndewura Jakpa made his capital. It was also a taboo for even the Sakpare Muslims, Fati Morukpe's descendants, to build a mosque in their quarters in Kpembe. It was only in about 1971 that the first two mosques were built in Kpembe, one by Kpembewura Abdulai Jawla Anabio and the other by the young men. Kpembewura Jawula Ababio did not use this mosque for more than two months because he had a stroke shortly after the construction of the mosque and was paralysed. People attributed this to the taboo. Of course, no elderly people prayed in these mosques, because of the taboo. It must also be noted that it was from Kpembe that Ndewura Jakpa marched to meet the Ashanti army from whose hands he met his death. If, therefore, he was the person buried in the mosque at Gbipe the people of Kpembe would not have considered it a taboo for their chiefs and princes to pray in a mosque or to taboo the building of a mosque in the town. Since Ndewura Jakpa is sacred to the Gonja people, the chiefs would have, without any reservation, worshipped his remains, which were buried in a mosque, instead of abhorring the mosque. There is another grave near the ruined mosque in Gbipe where Jakpa is said to have been buried called "Nyippe" (Master). The question is "who was the Master?"

The whole story of Ndewura Jakpa's burial at Gbipe and the Gbipewura's role as guardian of his tomb and the taboo forbidding the Yagbongwura (a descendant of Lata Jakpa) and the Gbipewura (a descendant of Manwura) meeting face to face, can be interpreted as a device of the traditional rivalry between Gbipe and Yagbong for the political dominance of the Gonja federation. However the Gbipewura is next to the Yagbongwura in seniority in the Gonja hierarchy.

---

33 "Lan ta" means the "Bow leader."

The Kuntunkure verse entitled "Kpa apo-che" (Discarder of the supposed weak army), which is the Executioner's appellation, shows the mood in which Lata Jakpa left Manwura. He said that "anger was to build a wall across their two states" and this means they were never to meet face to face again. The literal translation of the verse is:

Discarder of the women [suppose weak] army,
Listen again;
The enemy [Manwura] has grasped and eaten [assumed the sovereignty];
What do I [Lata] want in your small farm [state]?
To be married to young serpents?
[They say] they [the Manwura's people] will fight!
They will fight on whose trail? The foolish Bur [Burre Manwura] sits
To hear of his mates greatness.
And he will come to hear
That the mate's [Lata's] state is surpassing him.
And anger will build a wall partitioning [the two states].
King Hyena, proud army;
King Hyena, open your ears and listen!
If a witch says she will not fear the Executioner,
The Executioner's knife will not fear executing her.

The Kagbapewura also does not meet the Yagbongwura face to face, although he represents the Gbipewura in the enrobement of a Yagbongwura. The Kagbapewura's duty is to instruct the Yagbongwura as he is seated on the Kishi (mound) for his enrobement and after saying what he has to say, he tells the dogtes (linguists) and Sakpare Mallams "enrobe him on my behalf." After saying this he turns his back on the Yagbongwura and leaves for home. He does not even go through the town of Nyanga where the Yagbongwura stays when he leaves the place of installation, but by-passes the town. As soon as the Kagbapewura leaves for the place of installation his people also leave Nyanga to wait for him on the road. It is after the Kagbapewura has left the scene of enrobement that the new Yagbongwura is enrobed.

The Gbipewura and the Kagbapewura sit on one skin and on one cushion when they meet and neither of them takes off his hat in greeting the other because they are equal in rank. This is because their predecessors, the first Gbipewura and the first Kagbapewura were twins. They were Jafa, (Al Hassan) and Mafa (Al Hussein) the paternal nephews of Manwura, who were still children at the time of Mallam Mohamed Labayiru's (Fati Morukpe) visit to Manwura.

CHAPTER 6
Tuluuwewura Abbass and the Supposed Interregnal Period 1697–1709

Ndewura Jakpa's son was dead and so his brother Limu succeeded him.[34] Limu reigned for only two months. One Saywura (Senyonwura Lannyo) succeeded Limu and ruled for only eight months. Because Ndewura Jakpa was buried at Gbipe, the Lata Ngbanya decided to make the town their headquarters also, and it was here that both Limu and Senyonwura Lannyo were installed Kings. Senyonwura Lannyo was driven out of Gbipe by the Ashantis who had installed Sulemana as their protégé.

Senyonwura Lannyo returned to western Gonja and built the town of Bur'wurpe between Senyon, Nyanga and Mankuma where he settled. He assumed the title of "Burlannyo," that is, "Burre Wura Lannyo," because he was not now in active control of the Gonjas as sovereign; he was retired.

Tuluwewura Abbass, who was the son of Lanta (Lata-Dii Ngoro Jakpa) became the leader of the Lata Ngbanya (Gonja) when Lannyo was driven out of Gbipe but he was not installed King.

When the Tuluwe chiefship was created the Tuluwewura (Abbass was the first Tuluwewura) was stationed at Binyalipe, a place not far from Gbipe, with instructions to keep an eye on the Gbipe sovereigns. These instructions have become the Tuluwewura's Kuntunkure appellation and the literal translation of the verse entitled "Ka lii Chari," meaning "Chari's vanquisher" is:

> [This is the] home of the deserted Ngbanya [Gonjas],
> Vanquisher of Chari.[35]
> Matters are pending,

---

34 Mahama, son of Abdulahi; Arabic manuscript. This may not be Limu who was the brother of Manwura.

35 Mahama, son of Abdulahi; Sulemana was also called "So'ara" (Chari) after his grandfather but was also called "So'ara Sulimanu."

And the commoner passes by;

You [Tuluwewura] settle near the powerful man,
And let the weak ones take to the corners

I, a comrade, have escorted you with pomp
And dignity,
And I have left you in the yard of execution;
Murder is near you.
If it is not near you,
Why do you raise your head to watch?
Murder is there!
You murderer,
Are you the only one who wants to be sovereign?
It is because there are many informants in the King's palace,
The cook [Chari Sulemana] pecks at him,
But cannot hurt him.

Not long after his assumption of the leadership war broke out between him (Abbass) and the chief of Longoro. The war lasted for twelve years. These twelve years covered the period regarded as an interregnum by western historians.[36] The chief of Longoro died in the war and Tuluwewura Abbass and his brother Bur'Lannyo were left in control of the Longoro state. Forty days after the death of the Chief of Longoro, Burlannyo also died and left Tuluwewura Abbass the sole leader of Longoro and the Lata Ngbanya.

Possibly the Mos of Longoro were fighting the Lata Ngbanya on the side of the Ashanti protegé Sulemana Jakpa who might have been described as the chief of the Longoro. We have learnt that Sulemana's predecessor, the Manwura was styled the "Mo-wura." With the end of the war with Longoro, and possibly the death of Sulemana Jakpa, Abbass was free to wage war on Buna (Gbona). Tuluwewura Abbass as leader kept power in his hands for many years without being installed as King. He proved a good leader and a brave fighter. Abbass is said to have surpassed all his other brothers in intelligence and was more handsome and more religious. He attacked Gbona, setting out from Gbipe, and conquered the town. "Guna (Gbona) is a large city; half way from Guna to the Gonja country is the town called Ghofe (Gbipe); it is a ten days' journey and there is a river in between."

Tuluwewura Abbass was hailed King on the very day that he destroyed Gbona. Abbass had a lot of booty at Gbona and he gave to his Mallam, one Sherif, a quantity of gold weighing twelve miskals in the

---

36 Ivor Wilks: "A note on the chronology, and origins of the Gonja Kings," *Ghana Notes and Queries No. 8*, January, 1966.

name of God and also distributed a hundred miskals of gold among other Muslims who were Mallam Sherif's followers.

After his return from the conquest of Gbona, Tuluwewura Abbass attacked Fula (Banda). He defeated the people of Banda. Abbass was finally installed as King and one hundred days after his installation "he was killed by the Tonawa (Ashantis). He was killed on the fifteenth day of the month Rabi el-awal in the Hegira year 1121," that is on the 25th day of May, 1709.

What is regarded as an interregnal period, from 1697 to 1709 was in fact a period of struggle for power between the Lata Ngbanya (Ndewura Jakpa's people) and the Manwura's group (the Manwule people) who then controlled the Longoro area—the Mo country.

Kpembewura Mahama Labayiru, who was also the son of Lata Jakpa succeeded Abbass as Yagbongwura. He reigned for only two and a half years and died. After his death, power was no longer concentrated in the hands of one person as sovereign and the different divisions of Gonja became semi-independent states under a loose federal constitution. The Yagbongwura became a titular head only.

The Gonjas of the Tuluwe and the Kpembe areas came to be known as the "Singbingebi" ("Sin gbing"—the barring Sins). They barred the Gbipe people and their Ashanti allies from having complete control of the Lata Ngbanya.

Gbipe was considered not safe as a Lata Ngbanya headquarters because of the Ashantis and so the headquarters was removed to Nyanga. Kpembe and Wasipe considered the place too far from their homes and therefore did not care to be Yagbongwuras when the Headquarters was removed to Nyanga.

YAGBONGWURA

Kandia, Kung, Tuluwe, Bole and Kusawgu succeeded to the Yagbong Skins in turn. Kpembe argued that they had the Burre skins with them and they are the Skins on which the Kpembewura sat and they would therefore not descend to sit on the Yagbong Skins which were given to the Yagbongwura by Ndewura Jakpa. The Burre Skins are the original skins on which both Lata Jakpa and Ndewura Jakpa sat during their reign.

According to the Damongo Kuntunkurewura Dangba the following were the Yagbongwuras when Nyanga became the permanent head-quarters and who were buried at Mankuma, including Bur'Lannyo who was the first of the sovereigns to be buried besides his sister Jafo Sonni the Mankumoua (Chieftainess of Mankuma):

Name of Yagbongwura	Division	Remarks
1. Bur'Llannyo	Senyon	A retired Yagbonwura who was buried beside his sister Jafo Sonni at Mankuma
2. Kankanga	Kandia	–
3. Safu	Bole	-
4. Kali	Tuluwe	–
5. Jakpa	Kusawgu	–
6. Nyantachi	Kung	Died about 1873.
7. Jau	Tuluwe	–
6. Pirku (Mahama)	Kusawgu	–
9. Kurbang (Seidu Dushi)	Bole	His death in 1890 resulted in the Samori war because of a dispute about the successor.
10. Pontonprong (Abudu)	Bole	Installed after the Samori war.
11. Lannyo	–	Was Seripewura. He was installed because no Divisional Chief was prepared to fill the vacancy when the British Administration was pressing for a Yagbongwura to be installed. Lannyo was the son of a Bole princess and a prince of Kung. He was an Echipibi.
12. Dangbonga (Mahama)	Bole	1918–1937
13. Banbana (Iddi)	Tuluwe	1937–1942
14. Singbing Lannyo (Soale)	Kusawgu	1942
15. Ewurbunyangso (Ewuntoma Mahama)	Wasipe	1942–

After the death of Mahama Labayiru the Yagbongwura as sovereign of Gonja had no standing army. The national army consisted of the temporary co-operation of divisional forces and there were only those that were made available. Consequently the Paramount Chief had no monopoly of physical force. The Yagbongwura keeps his position of reverence and awe because he is regarded as a deity and the direct representative of Ndewura Jakpa whose spirit is believed to live in him. The Skin of Yagbong was a quasi-sacred office which was hedged with prohibitions. Like the Burre Kingship it became an "emeritus" office to be held in retirement by the "father" of the state at certain periods. The Yagbong Skins in the past usually lay vacant for many years for it was not an office which any one envied or wanted to occupy.

All the Divisional Chiefs call the Yagbongwura "father," even though he is not their putative father and all sub-chiefs call him their "grandfather." A Divisional Chief who is a brother of the Yagbongwura will address him, or refer to him, officially as "my father" and not "my brother." This description or designation of the Yagbongwura as "father" by the Divisional Chiefs has its origin in the first Divisional Chiefs being the sons or nephews of Lata Jakpa.

CHAPTER 7
The Gbipewura and the Kagbapewura

When Sulemana Jakpa died, the Gbipewura became the Wurkong (non-active Regent) whilst effective control of the state was in the hands of Tuluwewura Abbass who was the de facto Regent until his enrollment as King in 1709. Gbipewura was the keeper of Jakpa's grave so he was revered by all the Gonja Chiefs. Abbass was killed by the Tonawa (Ashantis) and his funeral was performed in Gbipe where all the chiefs assembled to elect a new King.

After the funeral Kpembewura Mahama Labayiru was elected and installed Yagbongwura. Gbipewura found his position weak because of the numerical strength of the Lata Ngbanya and he therefore conceded defeat. He had to say something[37] to the new King during his installation, but because he was angry and disappointed he would not go personally to talk to him and therefore sent his twin brother, the Kagbapewura to go and deliver his instruction. The Gbipewura's appellation in the Kuntunkure drum verses, is entitled "Dinkeri Wam-mu" (Dinkeri, Head of Wam's family). He the Gbipewura was now like the king of Denkyera who was defeated by the Ashantis who were formally subjects of the Denkyeras. The literal translation of the verse is:

> I am [now like] Dinkeri,[38]
> [I am]
> The head of Wam's family.
> I return to towns [to reconquer] as the feminine Chari [Sulemana] did.
> When my deceased grand-uncle slackened,
> His comrade was the Black-smith [Jakpa], the Dagomba Dey.

---

37 What is said at the installation of a chief is called "*Kante.*" They are instructions from the other chiefs, women chiefs and princes to the chief tell him how to behave and reminding him of his responsibilities towards them.

38 The Denkyira were defeated by the Ashantis in 1699 during the reign of Ntim Gyakari. Osei Kwamin Panin who reigned from 1781 to 1779 was the King of Ashanti.

> It was his [my grand-uncle's] comrade
> Who crushed him into powder.
> He who had heard what had happened[39]
> Is envious.

"Kagba pe wura" means "chief of the town of rebuke." He also rebuked the Lata Ngbanya. His Kuntunkure drum appellation, entitled "Wa peleng" (that which the Hyena [Chari] had burned [destroyed])" gives an idea of the mood in which he was. The translation of the verse is:

> It is the successor who recounts
> What the Hyena had destroyed.
> It depends on succession based on princeship
> And much depends on now.
> Will a stranger [the Lata Ngbanya] come to administer you?
> What then would you say to the one who is qualified?
> It is the person who is qualified
> Who opens his mouth
> To inform the one who comes today [*Ka ba mbare*—a
> stranger or immigrant]
> "It was at Long-po [Longoro] that he [the Kagbapewura]
> Went and saw Bori the hunter [warrior].
> He [the Kagbapewura] was then young playing
> Outside the compound and sitting on people's thighs.[40]

> The food [chiefship] that I [the Kagbapewura] will eat [assume]
> And suffer no pains,
> Is that which I will eat [succeed to],
> And my enemies hear of it—raise opposition.
> Damn my enemies!
> The patient one does not hasten
> The one who pulls down walls [who tumble sovereigns].

It is the duty of the Gbipewura to send the Kagbapewura to install the Yagbongwura when he is informed by the Senyonwura, who becomes Regent on the death of the Yagbongwura, that a new Yagbongwura has been elected. The Gbipewura has no power to disapprove of the candidate. He is informed of the date the installation is to take place.

On the arrival of the Kagbapewura in Nyanga, he becomes the most senior chief and everybody pays obedience to him. He does not call the

---

39 The Gbipewura was young when Manwura was reigning.

40 This confirms the record in the Arabic manuscript that Jafa and Mafa, the paternal nephews of Manwura, were still children at the time of Mallam Mohamed Labayiru's visit to Manwura.

Yagbongwura elect "Yagbongwura." He calls him by his Divisional Chiefship title such as "Bolewura" or "Kusawguwura" or "Tuluwewura," etc.

When a Yagbongwura dies the Senyonwura sends to the Gbipewura the deceased chief's horse, which is driven unsaddled and it is not ridden, his staff and sandals, to announce the death formally. The Divisional chiefs are also informed that "the tether-post is uprooted." They all then assemble at Nyanga or the headquarters for the funeral. After the seventh day funeral all the Divisional Chiefs meet under the presidency of the Senyonwura to elect a successor. When a successor is elected he is given the twelfth day funeral to perform. The Yagbongwura-elect then chooses the day on which he wants to be installed. The day of his installment must be after the performance of the twelfth day funeral. The Senyonwura then sends a linguist (dogte) to inform the Gbipewura of the candidate who had been elected and the day fixed for the installation. The Gbipewura then deputes the Kagbapewura to go to Nyanga and install the new paramount chief.

On his arrival the Kagbapewura takes precedence over the Senyonwura, although he remains the Regent, until the installation has taken place. At about 4 a.m. of the morning of installation the Yagbongwura's gun-men, who are his body-guard, will take arms and surround the mound ("kishi") on which the Yagbongwura is installed. The kishi is about five hundred yards west of the town. This is to prevent any prince getting access to it and sitting himself at the time of the installation. Any person eligible to the Yagbong Chiefship other than the Yagbongwura-elect, who is found sitting on the kishi at the appointed time of the installation must be enrobed as Yagbongwura without question and it is for this reason that precautions are taken. This custom has its origin from the time of the founding of the Gonja Kingdom as people had to fight to become Yagbongwura and it is the victor who gets himself installed as paramount.

There is a popular legend that one sub-chief of Tuluwe was elected the Tuluwewura. On the day appointed for his installation whilst he was getting his head shaved for the installation, his younger brother was also having his head shaved in his compound without the elder brother's knowledge. By the time the elder brother was ready to come out of his compound for his installation, the younger brother had already presented himself and was installed the Tuluwewura and he took the title of "Joro."

We may have some guide to this legend by studying the Tuluwewura's Mbontokurbi appellation. The appellation is for every Tuluwewura. The drum verses are like the national anthems to nations, no matter which is sovereign, or what party is in power, they remain the same. If we bear in mind that Sulemana Jakpa tried to usurp Ndewura Jakpa who had to be called home by the Dibirwura from his campaigns in the north country—the Dagomba land, and that Abbass who was the first Tuluwewura fought against Sulemana Jakpa in their struggle for power, we can best understand why precautions had to be taken to guard the kishi on which the Yagbongwura is installed on the morning of the installation of the new Yagbongwura.

The Mbontokurbi verse referred to is entitled "Joro" ("Jo lo" [wait, be quiet]). The literal translation is as follows:

> Chorus:
>   The claimant is alighting!
>   The claimant is coming!
>   Wait, be quiet,
>   The suicidal army.
>   "He is known to be on the verge of confiscation.
>   The dog kob [stag] of men!
>   Joro has offended the Dagomba Dey;[41]
>   The first to be struck (i.e., the Dagomba Dey),
>   Should bury the self-installed [usurper].
>
>   Wait, be quiet;
>   They are in conflict.
>   One says "I am Joro—the quiet waiter"
>   [There is also] Joro—the quiet waiter—the Dagomba Dey.
>
>   Joro the usurper
>   Who, when his elder brother was being shaved
>   [in preparation for his installation as the King],
>   And before his elder brother came out,
>   [For his installation]
>   He had installed himself as the king.
>   Joro has offended the Wan Dey [Dagomba Dey]
>   This is usurpation.
>
> Chorus:
>   The Claimant is alighting!
>   The Claimant is coming!

On the day of the installation of a Yagbongwura the divisional Chiefs and sub-chiefs, including princes who can aspire to the paramountcy, are not allowed near the kishi. Only the elders (Binimu) and Chamberlains (Bingbangpo) are allowed to be near it. The Divisional Chiefs, together with their sub-chiefs and princes sit about three hundred yards away from the place of installation.

---

41 All the lands conquered by Ndewura Jakpa, from Kapuyase to Bole and the countries around Wa were under the Dagomba Kings and therefore Dagomba land. Ndewura Jakpa became king of those lands after he had conquered them.

After the Kagbapewura has made his speech of instructions (*kante*) and has left the site, the Divisional Chiefs are called one by one in order of their seniority to go and make their speeches. As soon as one finished he returns to where his colleagues are seated before the next person is called. When the Divisional Chiefs present have all made their speeches, the elders are called upon to appoint a representative to make a speech on their behalf. They are followed by a representative of the Bingbangpo (Chamberlains) and then the women-chiefs (B'wurche). It takes about two hours to finish making the installation speeches.

After the speeches the Yagbongwura is enrobed by the linguists (dogtes) assisted by the Sakpare Muslims. The new Chief then rides on a horse with only the horse blanket on it. The horse is not saddled. After he has gone half-way between the kishi and where the Divisional Chief and their sub-chiefs are assembled, the Divisional Chiefs meet him and hold the bridle-rope of the horse ("kabarga"). The next Divisional Chief, in order of succession holds the bridle-rope nearest the bridle. The second in order of succession also holds the bridle rope after him and so the next until they all hold the bridle rope. They all then lead the horse and its rider, the new sovereign, a few yards home-ward before letting go the bridle rope. The chamberlains then take charge and bring the Yagbong-wura home.

After the exchange of greetings the Yagbongwura goes into seven days confinement. On the eighth day he comes out of his confinement and makes his policy statement. The Divisional Chiefs then ask leave of the Yagbongwura and return to their respective homes with their follow-ers. Their next visit to Nyanga may be when another Yagbongwura is to be elected and installed.

The last to leave will be the sub-chief from the Yagbongwura's original Division. After staying a few days to keep him company and for the appointment of a successor to fill the vacancy he had made by his installation as Yagbongwura, they also beg leave of him to return home. The successor is installed at the capital of his division.

The Yagbongwura is now left in his new home with only the mem-bers of his family and the elders who serve his office. He is now a stranger in a new home, surrounded by new chamberlains.

CHAPTER 8
The Salaga Market

The most important trading centre in Gonja during the early years of the Gonja settlement was Gbipe. Due to the unsettled state of affairs in the Gbipe area, owing to the constant attacks by the Brongs of Tachiman, the Nkoranzas and the Ashantis, people from other regions were reluctant to trade at Gbipe. There were traders from Hausaland to the Gbipe market. The Gbipe market was moved to Salaga when Gbipe's importance diminished. However, during the late 1800s the Gbipe market had somewhat recovered and people from other countries were trading there.

It was Ndewura Jakpa who brought the Nchibulungs as captives, refugees and mercenaries from the west, from the Banda area.

As he progressed in his adventure, Ndewura Jakpa recruited mercenaries from the conquered and subdued areas. Some of the refugees chose to follow him. The heads of many of these different tribes were honoured with offices of Mbongwura (war captain) or Egbangbo (Chamberlain) and were attached to his court.

Some of the Nchibulungs can be found in the Tuluwe Division. The majority of them were brought to Kpembe and put under Gonja chiefs. The Singbingwura is in charge of the Nchibulungs of the Chinke, Chachai and Banda groups, whilst the Kilibuwura was given charge of the Songhai group. The Songhai group comprises the people of the villages of Longo, Kpajai and Tamkulonku. The name Songhai was no doubt given the area in commemoration of the Gonja association with the Songhay Empire. The Kilibuwura is an important chief in the Kpembe hierarchy and he becomes the Regent on the death of the Kpembewura. One must be installed Songhaiwura before he is installed Kilibuwura. There is also the woman-chief with the title of "Songhaiwurche."

In the very early years of the Gonja settlement in Kpembe, the Kilibuwura was stationed at the town of Kuli and he had under his command 300 horsemen. His duty was to prevent traders from crossing the Volta River to go to Ashanti to either sell their merchandise or buy kola at a cheap price there. All persons were to come to Salaga to do their trading. Persons who wanted to force their way into Ashanti to trade had their merchandise confiscated and they were either killed or sold into slavery. They became "trade casualties."

It was for the purpose of opening the trade route which ended at Salaga that brought the Ashantis to invade Kpembe in 1744. It was during the reign of Kpembewura Isanwurfo Soale. He lost his life during the Ashanti invasion and his grave is to be found in the Salaga market. This was to honour him because he died in defense of the market. Sacrifices are made to the Isanwurfo grave annually by the reigning Kpembewura but this is not now strictly observed, because of economic difficulties.

As a result of the activities of the Kali people (who "gathered and ambushed" traders) which led to the establishment of the once famous Salaga market, Salaga became the centre of seven high roads. They were the:

1. Salaga to Kpembe road,
2. Salaga to Kotokoli road,
3. Salaga to Krachi road,
4. Salaga to Kintampo road,
5. Salaga to Bole road,
6. Salaga to Daboya road, and
7. Salaga to Yendi (Dagomba)—Hausaland road.

These roads gave Kpembe, the capital of the Kpembe Division its name of Agbambi (Roads) which has been corrupted to "Kembi." The Gonjas were able to achieve in Salaga, the direction of a trade route to where they wanted trade to be centred, what they failed to achieve in Begho, the prevention of Ashanti gold being sent to the sea coast and sold to European traders.

Trade was not unknown in northern Ghana before the advent of the Gonjas. For many centuries northern Ghana has been a meeting point of two great currents of external influence. The one descending southwestward from Hausaland, lake Chad and beyond, the other coming down in south-easterly direction from the Upper Niger. Here, for centuries, the two streams have met and mingled together until they have become almost indistinguishable. This kind of process, moreover, is carried forward largely by trade and by quite minor population movements. It would not be easy to relate it to rise and fall of states and dynasties even if we had a reliable political record.

By the same token, it must not be assumed that all traces of Mande influence either in Gonja or more generally in northern Ghana, are to be accounted for by Jakpa's invasion. For two hundred years or more preceding that invasion the trade routes which led to the Mandingo country on the Upper Niger had constituted Ghana's principal links with the wider world. By way of these routes the whole north-west of the country was penetrated by Julas, Ligbis and other Mandeised elements who came to make up an influential part of the population at every important trading centre and to play a key role in the advancement of Islam.

Already, before the age of Jakpa, Mande communities had arisen at Wa, Bono and Bole, all of them places on the trade routes to Northern Ashanti where the Mande trading settlement of Beawu (Begho), founded perhaps in the fourteenth century, was now at the height of its prosperity.

It was the geographical position of the district lying across the trade routes which led from Ashanti, north-westward to the Mande lands of the Upper Niger and north-eastward across Borgu to Hausaland which made Gonja a key region in the economic life of the western Sudan and which made the rise of effective state organisations there not only possible but necessary. According to the traditions of Bono-Mansu, alluvial gold was worked in the neighbourhood (at Wasipe) in the later middle ages and quickly became the occasion of commercial ties with countries of the north. This was why the Wasipewura who now resides in Daboya was stationed at Wasipe, a town south of Bole.

The forest of northern Ashanti also produced the red kola-nut (Steculia acuminata) always one of the staple commodities of long distance Sudanese trade. It is significant that the earliest known reference to Gonja, which occurs in the Kano Chronicle (Palmer, 1928, p. 109), indicates that the kola trade had brought Hausa merchants into this district as early as the middle of the fifteenth century. The Muslims whom Ndewura Jakpa met at Kafaba claim to have come from Hausaland and some of them were said to be Beriberi from Hausa. There was a trade route passing from the north and northwest to Ashanti through Kafaba.

Some traditions say that the name Gonja originated from the Hausa expression of "Zaa ni gun ja goro," meaning "I am going to the place of the red kola nuts." "Gun ja" (at the place of the red) was picked out of the sentence to give the people the popular name Gonja. The Gonjas call themselves Ngbanya; "ngba n nya" means "obtain my rebuke." It is also said that when the Gonjas (Mandingos) were setting out on their expedition they were told "ar gbanya, tag jona kana jona," meaning "be quick, go quickly and return quickly." Unfortunately, they did not return to Songhay, neither have they returned to Mande.

When a Gonja dies, and the grave is being dug, the hoe and axe used in the digging are held in the left hand and pointed to the east, south, north and west and the person doing so says "take them to K'Mande." To the Gonjas Mande is now the hereafter, and no one knows where the hereafter is.

Appendix I
Sulemani Kpatakpari

Sulemani Kpatakpari[42] is mentioned in three different songs in Gonja. During the damba ceremony the women singers call "Sulemani Kpatakpari to come out and dance damba," at about 4 a.m. that is the time Kpembewura is expected to come out of his compound to take part in the dancing.

The Dagomba drum beaters will give any chief whose name is Sulemana the appellation of Sulemana ben Dawudu (Sulemana son of Dawud). It is of course, difficult to say what connection Sulemana had with Askia Dawud who dispatched Mandinka cavalry, the founders of present Gonja, to Bono Manso to see what could be done about stopping the Akan gold-producers from selling some of their production to Portuguese and other European traders along the seaboard.

1. KPANA

Kpanaliumni is the Gonja hunters dance which is performed when a hunter kills a big animal such as the roan, hartebeeste, buffalo, lion or leopard, or when a great hunter dies. Kpana can be said to be the funeral dance of a reputed hunter. "Hunter" is a metaphor for "warrior" in the Kuntunkure drum verses. The Kpana dance is opened by the song "Sulemani salamalaikum" (Sulemana Salutations). Most Gonja songs are in proverbs and so are the Kpana songs. The literal translation of Sulemani salamalaikum is as follows:

> Sulemana offers salutations;—by soloist
> Saluations are unwelcomed—Chorus
> It is a stranger who is called "some body;"
> Salutations are unwelcomed.

---

42 In western Gonja trap is called "*kpatakpari.*"

He [Sulemana] is his mother's gold piece;
Salutations are unwelcomed.
If you don't want it, give it to his mother.
He is a Dagomba of Yendi
Ne does not understand Gonja;
Wulaa [what you say] is what he understands;
The K'gbatagbil[43] [waist beads] usually fits its owner;
In his case it does not fit;
It is a wise person who scares a fool;
A broken yam joins the rank of children;
He is the great bridle which tames the young horses;
The itching worm, he causes the backs of children to itch,
[He is] the burning sun that drives away the farmers.
Everything wants a companion;
The Katunpani [talking drum] is an exception;
The frog of the pit hole;
It is only on the day it rains that people hear
its recitations;
If you stand on a flat roof and find a lost slave,
You must sympathise with the pit [from which mortar was got for the building of the house].
The orphan, what has he got to say.
Each stanza is sung by a soloist and answered by the chorus
"Salutations are unwelcomed."

2. ALOBI

Another song in which Sulemani is mentioned is the song of the Alobi[44] dance which is performed by the women. The literal translation of the song is:

Sulemani has fallen,
let us cooperate to raise him
Sulemani, dwarfish respect,
Who surrendered to the grinding stone and later surpasses.
The Kiilinji [shade tree] that becomes the front of the house.
I have had an old experience.
The great barrier that bars the advance of the small fishes;
Ede fule—the fire lies; (the grass will grow)
Things do not grow on the wings [shoulders].[45]
It is because of death that teasing is painful,
Fear a person.

---

43 "*K gba Ata gbil*" means "rebuke Ata (the twin) and become blunt."

44 "*A lo ibi*" means "quieten the prince."

45 Sovereignty is not obtained by strength (but by heredity).

3. TAWARA

In the songs of the tawara dance, which is performed by the Mmara women of Larabanga, Sulemani is mentioned. According to Larabanga-wura Sidiki it was the Chafawura (Chefijiwura) who brought the Mmara from Mamprussi to work charms for him to win his wars.

Larabanga was noted as a place of Ashanti pilgrimage. Hundreds of years ago the Ashanti solicited the muslims of Larabanga to pray for them so that they could win their wars. Although the ancestors of the Ashanti muslim Community (Ashanti Kramo or Mbonto-sua as they are known by the Gonjas) came from Gbipe, "the head of the community, the Asante Adimen (i.e., al-imam) has as his symbol of authority a prayer skin said to have descended from the sky at Da'aban. Da'aban is the Twi rendering of Larabanga, the name of a town in western Gonja of great importance in the eighteenth century as a centre of Islam, which was reputedly carried there by "an Arab from Mecca."[46]

The people of Larabanga are called Mmara; the word may have been derived from the Arabic word "amara" meaning "command." The Mmara were then with the Nayiri of Mamprussi. The literal translation of the tawara song is:

> Sulemani Kpatakpari
> The woman who gave birth to Sulemani,
> Has indeed given birth to a great child.
> Kpatakpari—the trap.
> Sulemani, child of the owner [rightful heir];
> The deceased woman hooked you
> And you continued reigning.
> Jong-bi[47]—the young slave
> The struggle that will always exist.
> The young slave
> The *kude* [food prepared from the flour of grains] was spoilt.
> As a result of the grains.
> The person with a hip,
> Have you a nicer hip than me?

---

46 Ivor Wilks, *The Northern Factor in Ashanti history*, p. 22 (Institute of African Studies, University of Ghana).

47 "Jong" is a Jula (Wangara) word meaning "slave."

The Customs, Constitution
and History of the Gonja People

by H.H. Tomlinson

Foreword

My purpose in writing this essay on the Gonjas has been to make available in one place all that is at present known about them, for there are no published works about the Gonjas and there is little absolutely reliable information about them elsewhere.

This being my purpose I have deliberately eschewed mere speculation and the building of theories, tempting though these might have been, and have confined myself to an exposition of fact. My main sources have been the district Record Books, Diaries and Files of Bole and Salaga, the historical manuscripts which I have included in the appendices and my own investigations in the field.

No fact from any source whatever has been reported in this essay that has not been thoroughly checked by me with local people reputed to be experts on tribal history and custom. Where two or more conflicting versions of an historic event or tradition have emerged during my investigations and it has not been possible absolutely to discount one or other of them, both have been included.

From what I have seen, there is at present little system in the spelling of place and personal names. In order to effect some sort of standardisation I have used the spelling of place names employed by the Gold Coast Survey Department in the 9th Edition 1949 of their Road Map—Northern Section, Scale 1/500,000 throughout my text as this spelling is on the whole less grotesque than that of the Census of Population 1948 Report and Tables or other publications. In the same way I have tried to employ a uniform spelling of personal names and titles. I have not, however, interfered with either the spelling or form of the manuscripts printed in the appendices save in Appendix XII, which I have arranged in paragraphs.

As regards the Notes to the History and to the appendices, I have tried to keep them to a minimum and to avoid repeating information that is given in a note elsewhere.

Finally, I must record my indebtedness to the Chiefs and people whose names appear in Appendix XIII for their help and for their patience in answering my many questions, to Mr. Jack Goody for allowing me to read the typescript of his "Ethnology of the Northern Territories of the Gold Coast" and to use some of the material contained in it, to Mr. A. Duncan Johnstone without whose pioneer work of collecting and translating the historical manuscripts in Appendices IX, X and XII, my task would have been made much harder, and to my Interpreters Soal Mama of Bole and Iddi Seidu of Salaga.

I need hardly add that mine is the sole responsibility for all that is written.

H.H.T.
Salaga, 5/2/54

The Languages and Peoples of Gonja

When the Gonjas invaded the country they found it inhabited by numerous tribes each speaking a slightly different language or dialect. They made them their subjects and gave them the collective name Nyamase (singular Kanyamase) which means "He has it but won't give it away unless he is forced to do so." The tribes that came into the country subsequent to the Gonja invasion, the Lobis for instance, are not included within the meaning of the word.

The Gonja rule was benevolent and the Nyamase were allowed to continue in their ownership of the land, possibly because the Nyamase knew the deities and ceremonial of the land cult which the invading strangers could not know. The Nyamase also retained their Priest Chiefs and continued to speak their own languages. In consequence all over Gonja, the newcomers adopted local words into the Gonja language which became broadly divided by slight differences of dialect and pronunciation. From this confusion of tongues I endeavoured, in 1952, in my "Gonja Grammar and Word List" to distil the pure essence of the Gonja language.

The importance of the Nyamase Chiefs and Priests in the Gonja political system is emphasised by the fact that every Divisional Chief except Kpembewura is enrobed by a Kanyamase Chief, and every Gonja Chief has the Chief of the local inhabitants as an important elder.

Here is a list of the tribes and languages of Gonja. In the West and Central Gonja, languages of three linguistic groups are spoken.

I. The Grusi group:

Vagella	in Sawla, Jentilipe, Grupe, Nakwaby, Tuna, Soomia, Jang, Mbolebi, Dabori, Degwiwu, Chorobang, Bole and Gelencon.
Choroba	in Seripe and Senyon.
Mo	in Fumbo and also in the Mo and North Mo States.
Tampluma	in Bugay, Konkori, Sala, Isalakawu, Bungweli, Mankariga, Lokuli, Yabum, Zantana, Goreba, Jinkrom, Nalori, Basampa, Nabengu, Denkerepe and Donkompi.

II. The Mossi group:

Dumpo	in Kalonso, Boakipe, Jembito and Bonipe.
Safaliba	in Mandare, Buanfo and Tankpe.
Nome	in Ypala, Pongeri, Kulmasa, Nahari, Kinchin and Sonyeri.
Batigi	in Kunfosi.
Mara	in Larabanga, Nabori and Dokrupe.
Anga	in Murugu, Busunu, Chutadi, Lankatere, Yarizori, speaking Kodengu, Kpalumbo (Kubeng), Jinfronu, Bowena and Tsakalia Anyanto.

III. The Senufo group:

Pantera	in Tinga and Wasipe (Bole Division)

Eastern Gonja

Nawuri	in Alfai area.
Nchumbulung	in Lonto, Padjae, Tankulanku, Ekumdipe, Bankamba, Chakori, Jimbupe (Sebon Gida), Kabesi, Kachanki, Kwadjobonae, Kuminiso, Krukruba, Nangjuri, Tori and Wiaye.
Dagomba	in Kusawgu area: Saggia, Busa and Zepe.
Mparaba	was spoken in Kakpande, Janton and Panshiaw but Dagomba has replaced it and the language is dead.
Mpara	was spoken in Kusawgu, Tuluwe and on the banks of the White Volta. The language is now dead.

DOMESTIC INSTITUTIONS AND CUSTOMARY LAW

The Gonja family is a larger unit than its British counterpart and consequently the family head is a man of considerable position. He succeeds to his position in this way. When the head of a family dies, his brothers may succeed in order of seniority before the men of the next generation become eligible. These take their rank in order of their birth and not from the seniority of their parents. Thus:

A, the head of the family dies, his brothers having pre-deceased him without issue. He has two sons *B* and *C* who each have two sons in this order: *B* (2 and 4), *C* (1 and 3). When *A* dies he is succeeded by *B*, on whose death *C* succeeds. After that the succession is 1, 2, 3, 4, in that order.

A

B   *C*

2 4 1 3

He has power over the members of his family whatever their age and is normally the only person who will be given the guardianship of a child.

Polygamy is practised in Gonja, though modern economic conditions make it unusual for a man to have more than two wives and may in time compel a state of monogamy. The marriage contract is easily made for the woman's consent is not necessary to the match. Her suitor must however win her parents consent, which he does by presenting them with kola nuts. If he has a brother, the brother makes the gift, it not, he does so himself. The girl's parents then take equal shares of the kola.

Vagella and Safaliba custom is similar save that instead of kola nuts an annual gift of a basket of millet is made to the girl's mother. If the gift is omitted for two years in succession the girl is taken back and presumed never to have married. Any children however, belong to the father.

If possible a man marries the child of his mother's brother or that of his father's aunt in the belief that he will be better looked after by a relative of his family than by an outsider. There is, however, no bar to his marrying outside the family circle. The cement of marriage is the gift of kola nuts and if this is absent then the concubine may leave her master when she wishes and he has no claim in cases of adultery. Children of such a liaison belong to their father, though if there are many, he may allow his concubine to take some.

As in England in earlier ages, a girl is recognised as marriageable as soon as she has her first menses. Boys do not usually marry until they are near their twentieth year. Marriages may be contracted to within the degree of first cousin. There seems to be no actual marriage ceremony as we know it, though on her wedding before she is given to her husband the bride is ceremonially washed. The ceremony is performed to the accompaniment of slow drumming and to the chanting of girls. The bride, who is surrounded by young girls, is supported by her sister, or if she has none, by a woman friend and by an old woman who holds her hand over the bride's mouth. All the while other people look on and make gifts of money, etc. That night the bride goes to her husband and the following night there is dancing and drumming in honour of the newlywed couple. Often the celebration goes on for several nights. If a man has more than one wife, then the one whom he married first is the head wife, a position that carries with it little authority. Each wife with her children occupies one room in the husband's compound if he can afford it.

Adultery may be compensated for by money paid to the outraged husband. Adultery by a man with his brother's wife is regarded as an offence not only against the living but against the dead who are buried in the compound where the offence was committed. In the old days the offender was ostracised from his family. For a divorce, the consent of the Divisional Chief is all that is required. Not unnaturally this rather lax attitude towards marriage is accompanied by an equally generous attitude towards illegitimacy which is barely regarded as a slur on either the bastard or its parents. Bastards always belong to their mother. There has never been any adoption of children.

The Gonjas circumcise their male children which may emphasise their connection with Islam in the past. Indeed when the marauding bands of Ndewura Jakpa were first seen by the Nyamase of Sakpa near Bole the startled locals remarked on the absence of foreskins on the naked boys of the invaders. The time of the operation, which is performed by the Isepo or barber, varies throughout Gonja. In the West it is done when the infant is a week old, in Kpembe when he is a month old and in Wasipe when the boy is seven years old. The skin is buried by the Isepo and the old woman who held the baby during circumcision. The child is shaved at the same time.

Before the coming of the British with their cemeteries and sanitary rules all Gonjas save Chiefs and Ewuriches, who had special burial places, used to bury their dead outside the walls of their compounds and mark the grave with an upright stone. Traditional methods of burial for men and women vary slightly. A man is buried in a cloth gown and his corpse lies on its right side and faces east with the head to the South. The corpse of a woman on the other hand faces West with its left hand on the ground and its right hand resting on its right cheek. The head lies to the South and care is taken that the corpse does not stiffen. The reason that a female corpse faces West is so that it can watch the sun go down at eventide, which as in life is the signal for the women to prepare the food and fetch water. The corpses of only children are given a particular treatment. They are buried beneath the roof gutters of the mud houses of Western Gonja or in the East by the washing place of their compound. If all such places are occupied, then a friend is asked to lend his *champulte* or washing place. These children are buried thus to ensure that in death they may always be amongst friends as during life they had no brothers or sisters. Their corpses are wrapped in raw cotton. The graves are dug to a depth of some five feet and are closed by a wooden door. They lie at right angles to their shafts which are filled up with earth and marked by an upright stone. The corpse is lowered head first.

The grave diggers are known as *Bechange Kurupo* (singular *Echang Kurupo*) and are responsible not only for the digging of the grave but for the burial of the corpse. The office is not hereditary and a would-be *Echang Kurupo* must pass an initiation test of being buried naked with a corpse for at least one hour in a closed grave. The inducement to this office is that a person thereby gains immunity against corpses which, unless medicine is immediately available, are believed to cause death to anyone who touches them. For their services the *Bechang Kurupo* are given one male goat.

Burial is usually performed within an hour after death for common folk or within twelve hours for Chiefs and notables. The celebration of the funeral, however, takes place three days after death for a man and four days after death for a woman. This is followed by celebrations on the seventh, twelfth and fortieth day after the death of a common person with a final celebration of the funeral custom a year after the death for a Chief. Women mourn a death by smearing ashes over their bodies, while men do so by attaching red strips to their clothes.

Legal ideas are fairly well developed amongst the Gonjas both appertaining to one man and his neighbour, and, more remarkably, between the individual and the State. In the civil law the conceptions of succession, property, inheritance and contract exist.

As we have seen, a man is succeeded by his brothers and sisters; then by his children and their children. Where there are twins the procedure is unusual for it is the last and not the first who is considered the elder and therefore the heir. His heirs male and female inherit his property including his widows who are free to contract new marriages. If there are neither brothers nor sons then the property goes to the head of the family, or if the dead man was a "stranger," to the Divisional Chief through the Local Chief. If a man dies without heirs his property descends to his family head (or in certain instances to Chiefs, one of whom is Kafabawura). It is incumbent upon a man's heirs to settle his debts and pay the cost of his funeral. The same rules of inheritance apply whether the deceased was sane or insane.

The property of a dead woman goes to her sisters or if there are none, to the deceased's elder child and if there are none of these, then to the head of her own family. The inheritor is in the position of a guardian of the property which he may either keep, loan or give away as he feels. Her husband has no control over it.

In the event of the death of an important Chief, property belonging to the skin, in contrast to his personal property, is taken care of by traditional custodians or by guardians appointed by the elders according to the local custom.

Property in land belongs to the Divisional Chiefs through the Kasale-wuras who are Chiefs of the Nyamase tribes which inhabited the country before the coming of the Gonjas, and to no others. Any encroachment on these land rights is punishable by the Chief though a pretty liberal view is taken in this empty land.

In contrast to rights over land a person may have rights to trees. Of course a man has the usufructuary rights of his farm. Even a slave in the old days had these rights though he was obliged to give a small amount of its produce to his master. Unlike the freeman, however, he could not pass on his rights to his descendants, for they automatically reverted to his master on his death.

On the whole land is not leased to strangers and farms are divided from one another by paths only.

Contracts in this non-literate society were verbal and made before witnesses. Enforcement could be had on application to the Chief and in the same way debts could be recovered.

All articles save wives and children could be bought and sold, but children could be pledged as security for debt, etc. Usury was not practised.

The offences which the Gonjas traditionally recognise as being criminal are those which I give in their order of turpitude:

Murder
Witchcraft
Theft
Gambling
Defilement of infants
Adultery with a Divisional Chief's wife
Adultery in the bush or farm
Stealing from a farm
Arson
Intercourse with an animal

Attempts to commit these crimes were regarded as meriting punishment in the same way as the committal of the crime itself.

Punishment in the old days was apt to be drastic but except in very serious cases was conjoined with payment of compensation for damage to the aggrieved party, just as in cases of seduction and adultery a money payment was made to the husband of the despoiled woman.

Murder and Witchcraft were punished by instant beheading, on the order of the Divisional Chief, if the offender admitted guilt and his severed head was displayed in a public place for all to see.

Theft, Gambling and Adultery with a Divisional Chief's wife were punishable by death on a second offence. For a first committal of the latter crime the man had to provide a cow in compensation and swear the "Ntang" oath on the Divisional Cushion not to do it again. The woman was whipped.

Defilement of an infant was punishable with death if the victim died in consequence of the rape. Otherwise payment of monetary compensation by the raper to the child's parents or guardian, as in the case of rape of a promised girl, would suffice.

Adultery in the bush or farm and Stealing from a farm were punished by public exposure and whipping. The offender was led naked round the town with a rope tied round his waist. Adultery in the bush or farm is also regarded as an offence against the land deities and the offender must give a sheep and a goat to the Kaselewura for sacrifice at the place where the offence occurred.

Arson and Intercourse with an animal were regarded as the acts of a lunatic and the offender was secured by the leg in a log bored for the purpose.

In cases of theft and gambling a first offender was put under the surveillance of the Begbangpo who also enquired if he had been found guilty of a previous offence of that nature.

Both civil and criminal causes were heard by the Chief and his elders on whose land the offence had been committed, and if the party or parties to a case were dissatisfied with the decision of this village court they could, by swearing the Divisional Chief's oath, have the case transferred to his court, in which case one or both parties would inform the Mbonwura who would thereupon arrest both parties and claim his fee Kagbon. If both women and men were involved in a case, then the village Ewuriche or the senior Ewuriche sat with the Chief; if between women only, the Ewuriche judged it alone; if over land then the Nyamase Land Priests were called in to advise the Gonja Chiefs.

Where the subject of another State committed an offence in Gonja, presents would be sent by the Gonja Divisional Chief on whose land the offence was committed, to the offender's Chief, who would give them to the offender's family. The family would normally apologise. The procedure was adopted because if justice were left to take its normal course war would probably have resulted.

It was the obligation of the head of an offender's family or the people of his village to hark him to justice.

At the trial, witnesses were sworn on fetish and afterwards the successful party gave the Divisional Chief a present in token of gratitude.

Religion and Custom

The Gonjas are still mostly pagan though in addition to Fetish Priests or Lissu, they brought Moslem Priests with them when they invaded what are now the Northern Territories, and though year by year Islam wins its converts, the pagan Gonjas believe in a supreme God whom they call "Ebori" which is the same word that they use for rain. Subordinate to him are a host of spirits having their habitations in woods and stones and teasing any mortal who may trespass upon their preserves without having first performed the proper ceremonies.

It is through the medium of the fairies to whom he talks, that the Ejo or Soothsayer gets his information. He may be of any tribe and is a very gay personality with his cloth belt and dress of cowries and his sprightly dancing. Gonja caution, however, decrees that he must tell fortunes before he has been in a village for a week lest local gossip and not the talking of the tree fairies becomes his guide.

The Gonja's revere ancestral spirits and believe in "Dead Bodies" or ghosts. The spirits of a Divisional Chief's predecessors are believed to answer the call of his drums on Mondays and Fridays and come to greet their reigning brother when their names are announced.

The Gonjas do not like to think that a person died a natural death so they seek to account for deaths by a belief that certain people can turn themselves into poisonous snakes and dangerous animals. But the belief does not stop there. For example if a hunter is killed by a wild animal in the bush, his relatives will try to find out who it was in the wild animal's skin. To do this they will consult an "Epalepo" or medicine man. (These men are wanderers and need not belong to any particular tribe.) The Gonja method of tracking down "werewolves" is for the enquirer to hold the base of the Ebalepo's stick while the latter holds its head. The enquirer talks the while mentioning the names of his suspects. Until the two agree upon a name they swing the stick back and forth, but when the true name of the suspect is discovered they bang the stick on the ground.

The Gonjas also believe in the "Evil Eye" and to protect their farms from it they take great precautions. If an ill-wisher says "What a fine farm that is" of a man's farm, the farmer must abstain from sexual intercourse that night and go to the farm early next day without talking to anyone, taking with him Ela medicine which everyone keeps hanging above the door of his room in a horn or shell. When he reaches the farm he chooses a stone (Ela Kajembo) which he marks with a black X. He makes no sacrifice, says nothing and does no work on the farm that day, but returns in silence to his home.

It is probably no exaggeration to say that every village, house and farm in Gonja has as its fetish some rock or tree, mud shrine, stream or prominent feature of the landscape, which is the abode of a spirit who must be placated or whose aid must be sought. Sometimes the fetish may be made known only to initiates who form a society bearing its name, or it may be famous far and wide and help diverse people with their problems, or as regards the fetishes of the hearth and of the farm may be known by the family of the local Land Priest respectively. When a man chooses a site for his farm he goes to the Kupo to have the necessary sacrifices made to the stone or tree where the spirit of his farm abides. Such sacrifices are repeated each year at seed time and harvest for first fruits.

The most respected and popular fetish in Gonja is *Senyon Kipo* which is situated at Senyon near Bole. It is a stone and is served by the "Tindana of Western Gonja" who is elected by the villagers from the Samape family. He is assisted by a man of the Bampaware family. Senyon Kipo is visited annually for the Den Festival by representatives of all villages where Gonjas live some coming from as far away as Ashanti. Everyone including the Yabumwura brings presents. Until the festival has been celebrated the people of Senyon are not allowed to farm. Debts to Senyon Kipo are settled by offering animals for sacrifice. No attempt is made to drive hawks from the Fetish site where they prey on the fowls gathered there which may mean that the Hawk is sacred to the Fetish.

Senyon is full of superstition. When I visited it on horseback in 1951, I was asked to dismount and leave my horse on the Bole side of the village because on the other side there is a tree which no horse may see and survive.

The *Malkunde Fetish* at Lamasa in the Tuluwe Division is known throughout the Northern Territories. It was brought originally from Kandiau in the Wala country. People came to it for aid particularly in cases of child birth.

The *Lasah Fetish* of Chama is a fertility and healing Fetish.

The *Tigari Fetish* is known throughout the Gold Coast as a protector of towns and as an aid to fertility in barren women. It is also reputed to be able to catch thieves, provide water, bring good harvests, and make weapons effective against witches. Ypala is the home of this Fetish which was discovered about 1903 by one Kakuro who handed on the secrets to his brother, Jarama. They devolved next to his younger brother, Kaluna, who in turned passed them on to his son, Tifo, the present Fetish Priest.

The *Sigma Fetish* originated in the Tampluma area, but now has followers in many villages of North Western Gonja. Sigma is a secret Society. Any member who has a complaint to make may go to the Fetish hut, don his vestments and thus disguised go round the village voicing his complaint. His anonymity is protected by the Fetish. When a prominent man dies, provided he has not offended the Fetish, the members of the Fetish, in his village, will put on their costumes and caper round the town. I saw such an exhibition at Sala in 1953 performed in honour of the Kupo (Land Priest) who had just died. Children may be initiated, a fact which is commemorated in the idiomatic description of a dwarf, "You are like Sigma's son."

The vestments of this Society, which are kept in a small thatched hut set apart from the village, consist of small black fibre skirts extending into pantallettes and made in one piece, a fuzzy wuzzy head-dress the front of which is formed by a wooden mask carved and painted in the likeness of a face. Each of the fetish villages has a different face carving. At Kunfosi it is a bush cow or a child; at Sala a harte-beast. Each member of the Fetish carries a short wooden baton in the right hand when he is dressed up.

In various ways certain villages in Gonja have become sanctuaries. Besides Buipe and the villages of the State Bagbangpo, the District Record Books mention Kafaba and Ka in Janton as being Sanctuaries. Kafaba was declared a sanctuary and its Chief was made a peacemaker by Ndewura Jakpa when he first came there. Ka is a sanctuary for runaway wives. It is connected with the Jalo Fetish which can dissolve marriages, the guardian of which is Karakpema, the Chief Kasalewura of Janton.

Besides the Fetishes, many of which are probably of pre-Gonja origin as they are intimately bound up with the cult of the land, there are certain definitely Gonja shrines and sacred objects. The most potent of these sacred objects are the two Alite which are red clay dwarf images given by Malam Fatu Morukpe to Burylanyon at the time of the division of the Kingdom. Burylanyon took the Alite with him to Bole and later to Nyanga when he was elevated to the Yabum Skin. It is said that one or both of the Alite was lost during the Samori Wars, but this is doubtful. The Alite are said to be kept secretly at Nyarwupe in the Kusawgu Division. This is supported by the fact that Yabumwura always stops there on his journeys to Yapei and gives gifts to the Enumu. In olden times these gifts were a white cow, a white sheep, and mats in which to wrap the Alite and other sacred objects. Now the gift is a white fowl and mats. The colour white is significant, for a white gift is a token of friendship and means a white heart. In olden times a black or a coloured gift would often be refused. The Alite are believed to be the source from which the Yabumwura's powers spring and their loss would be regarded as a disaster in the tribe. So great is the force emanating from these images that Yabumwura has to give each of them a new white gown every six months as the previous one will have been burnt through. Mallam Fatu Morukpe is said also to have derived some of his powers from them. So his gift to Burylanyon was indeed a princely one.

Ndewura Jakpa's grave at Buipe is the tribal shrine of the Gonjas and a sanctuary for malefactors. It is a long barrow like mound situated on the side of the Morno path opposed to the Rest House. Tradition records that the mound was once high and fenced about with stakes brought thither and maintained by Ashantis. Now its appearance is insignificant. Naturally this shrine is the subject of many superstitions. One concerns the annual bush burning which is started by the Buipewura in person. If the fire burns over the grave it is held to be a bad omen for the year and it is believed that the man who started the fire will die. If on the other hand the fire stops before reaching the grave it is supposed to signify a prosperous and happy year. The precaution of weeding the grave is taken before the date for bush burning is fixed.

Of all the Gonja Festivals the most important is Damba. It is celebrated by each of the Divisional Chiefs, the Yabumwura and certain other privileged Chiefs in their own villages. This is a reversion to the original practice, for there was a time during the 1930s when all the Divisional Chiefs and their Limans were ordered into Nyanga to celebrate the Feast with Yabumwura.

The Festival follows a similar plan in all the Divisions with the exception of Kpembe which follows Dagomba practice of celebrating a Small Damba on the twelfth–seventeenth days of the Damba Moon and a Great Damba on the thirteenth day of the Moon. It is a time of general licence. As I was lucky enough to see three Dambas in Bole (1950–52), I will give a detailed description of the procedure there. Afterwards I will note any variations that I know of in other Divisions.

The beginning of Damba is marked by the Rice Picking Ceremony which is held in Bolewura's compound under the directions of Seripewura who is the master of ceremonies. Rice is spread out on a mat in front of the Bolewura. Then to the accompaniment of drumming and thrice repeated prayers by the Moslems, the "chaff" is picked from the grain in three successive operations. When this is done every Chief present takes one grain of rice which he keeps. When he dies these rice grains are counted and his years of Chiefship are calculated from the number of Dambas he celebrated. Now the Mbontosua of Maluwe give Bolewura a customary present of kola nuts in token of long friendship between their ancestors and the early Gonjas. Before handing over the gift the chief Mbontosua eats one nut to show that the nuts are not poisoned. Finally any of the Chiefs or Princesses present who wish, may perform a solo dance, their robes being held up by male relatives and their faces being fanned by their women who dance in retreat before them.

On the morning of the second day two sacrificial cattle are slain. One is given to the "ancestors"; the other, which is slaughtered outside the Bolewura's compound is given to the Moslems. The bull for "ancestors" lies trussed to a log inside the compound. Immediately before it is slain,

Bolewura and his Chiefs and the Liman and his followers file round it in a wide circle. After every four paces the procession pauses while the Moslems recite verses from the Koran. This over and the Moslems having retired Bolewura goes up to the bull, dips his fingers in water and runs them over the bull three times from snout to tail. He then dances to his place greeting the Liman on the way. The Muezzin now kills the bull by cutting its jugular vein and drums beat the while. Pots are placed to catch the first flow of blood. Then the beast is left to its death throes and its bleeding slowly crimsons the soil. Finally the Moslems offer prayers for Bolewura, after which the day is given up to drinking. This is the great night of the festival. Dancing starts at moon rise in Bolewura's compound, but after a while the dancing Chiefs and people move outside where they continue to dance until dawn, visiting every section of the town.

On the third day at daybreak, Bolewura who has been keeping vigil in his compound comes out in state, clad in his hooded gown with his Counsellors, Mbonwura and gunmen. He dances one circle of Damba while guns are being discharged. He then sits on his skins and cushion and for a few minutes watches the revelry which daylight has made to look rather tawdry. After this he returns to his compound.

In the evening before sundown the final rites of Damba are performed. A great assembly of Chiefs and people gather and the Liman, preceded by his Muezzin and Dabo come to their seats followed by Bolewura and his retinue. Now the food which has been prepared by the Ewuriches from the slaughtered cattle and gifts of grain given by the Chiefs is brought and placed in the arena ready for distribution by Nangbewura (the archer). He apportions the food in the customary way between people from other Divisions, to Walas living in Bole, to Mbontosua, to Ntere, to "thieves" and to "any others." In 1951 the distribution of food was upset because a woman stepped out and claimed a share. She was the daughter of a slave which status gave her the right to ask any favour of Bolewura which he must grant her.

The food having been distributed by Ngangbewura prayers are said by the Moslems for the welfare of Bolewura and his division. Then in olden times the Ntere performed their traditional mimic dance in which a cow's shoulder blade is used to symbolise a paddle. Now only Nangbewura comes out to do his traditional dance pretending to shoot enemies with his leopard skin covered bow. If the arrow is accidentally let fly, bad luck is supposed to come to the Division.

Next the assembled Chiefs pay homage. To do this they walk in file in a circle and on the orders of the dogte (spokesman) remove their caps and repeatedly prostrate themselves on their left sides until the Nsawura is satisfied. Any Chief who fails to make a proper obeisance is noticed by the dogte who announces his shortcoming to the crowd and thereby makes him a laughing stock. Bolewura uses the occasion of homage to address a little homily to the assembly on current topics and on governance generally. The homage of the Chiefs is followed by that of the Ewuriches (Princesses) and their dogtes. The Ewuriches do homage by prostrating themselves on their right sides at the order of the Nsawura, but their dogtes go down on their hands and knees. When this is over Bolewura returns to his compound. The crowd disperses and Damba is over for another year.

The programme at Kpembe shows some variation, on the eleventh day of the Damba Moon Kpembewura chooses sacrificial cattle in the presence of his elders and Salagawura. One is then slaughtered and the other is given to Soma (a Moslem Elder of Lamporowura) who lives in Salaga. Soma accompanied by Salagawura, the Kpembewura's representative, goes to Salaga where the ox is killed and the meat is divided and distributed. In the afternoon rice is picked and pounded ready for cooking at Kpembe and Salaga. Throughout the night there is drumming and dancing until dawn and the Kpembewura's Chiefs assemble in his compound to receive small portions of the cooked rice to eat and to take home. In Salaga the Salagawura and his elders visit Soma's compound for the same purpose.

In the morning of the twelfth day, all the Salaga people go with Soma to Kpembe where he and Kpembewura each give one small calabash of cooked rice and meat to the Kpembe Liman who prays over the food and takes it to his compound for himself and for his family to eat. This is the principal ceremony of Sinyani, or little Damba.

Nothing more happens until the morning of the sixteenth day of the Moon when rice is prepared at Kpembe in the compounds of Kpembewura and his Gate Chiefs; of Lepowura, the Liman and Kawasiwura; also in Soma's house in Salaga. The populace visits these compounds in the order of their owner's seniority to help to pick rice and to be given a little.

Next morning everyone again repairs to Kpembe for the killing of the cattle. This done they return home, the carcasses are cut up and the meat is distributed to the Chiefs and elders, and to the Liman who receives one foreleg together with the offal. Soma does not kill anything on this occasion. In the course of the day Kanakulaiwura, Kawlawura and Kilibiwura send a swift messenger to Kpembe with a present of one hind leg of beef from each of them. The messenger is given a piece of meat as a reward for his services. At night the women prepare the meat and pound rice.

On the eighteenth morning of the moon, in the presence of the people of Kpembe, Kpembewura, his Gate Chiefs, Lepowura, Kawisiwura, and Liman, Niami, and Soma each place in the arena one calabash of rice with a piece of cooked meat on top of it. The Liman offers prayers. Then young girls place the calabashes on their heads and dance in a circle followed by anyone else who wishes to dance. When the dance is done and the calabashes of food have been replaced on the ground the Niami calls a young man to take one calabash of food and place it before the Liman. He then takes one for himself and after that any youngster may take a calabash of food and give it to his Chief. In the olden days however, these calabashes were earmarked for Sisi, the drummers and Male the descendants of an old Hausa of that name whom Ndewura Jakpa met in Salaga. This over the people disperse.

The nineteenth morning marks the end of the Damba festival. The Chiefs, elders and Liman assemble in Kpembewura's hall where they are given food, which meal is called Kajipa. When they have finished eating, water is brought for them to wash their hands. The Liman then offers prayers and kola nuts are handed round. Finally the assembly thanks the Kpembewura and disperses home.

The variations of the Great Dambas of the 1930s held at Nyanga were these. On the first day when the rice had been spread on a mat before the Limans, portions of the rice were put in brass bowls by the dogtes and distributed into the hands of each Chief for cleansing. The Limans then gathered round the mat and chanted prayers eight times and drummers played in the intervals of prayer. The rice was then taken back from the Chiefs, replaced on the cloth and given to the Ewuriches to the accompaniment of more drumming.

After solo dancing and prayers for Yabumwura's welfare and for general prosperity, the Chiefs formed a circle for their act of homage. Then the Mbonwura greeted the Yabumwura but did not remove their caps like the Chiefs. They were followed by their gunmen who were dressed in hunting attire. Finally the Ewuriches did homage.

On the third day there is no record that the Yabumwura came from his compound at sunrise.

Like Damba, the Festival of the Guinea Fowls is said to be of Moslem origin. It is held yearly in the month of Kachanjiful and this is the Gonja legend of its origin. Long ago while a war was being waged, water became so scarce that warriors were dying of thirst and the fighting was held up. A guinea fowl saw the plight of the warriors and flew to where there was water, dipped his feathers in it and returned to mock the warriors by flapping his wings and splashing them with drops of water. They asked the guinea fowl to show them the water, but he refused. So they cursed him. Not long after the warriors saw a bush pig whom they asked to show them the water. He replied "Follow me," and led them to a river where all the people drank. They blessed him for his help. That is why to this day Moslems and all reigning Gonja Chiefs refrain from eating Bush pig, and why every year in this month the people take a guinea fowl and while it is still alive pluck its feathers and beat it with a switch cut from a *dawa* tree to punish it for its ancient perfidy.

Another important Gonja Festival which is probably common to the whole of Gonja is Jintigi, Ambatigi or Jumbenti as it is variously called. It is a village ceremony in which the people dance with lighted grass torches in their hands. The dancing is followed by ceremonial cleansing in water provided by the Chief and blessed by the Liman. This Festival falls at the beginning of the dry season.

It is remarkable that in all the so-called Gonja Festivals the Liman and his Moslems play such an important part. Perhaps Moslem Festivals were adopted at the expense of Gonja ones. This might account for the disappearance from Salaga of the Isanwurupe Ceremony which was very confused in its performance in 1935 and is now no longer known.

The Festival of New Yams, Gbangdawu, contains another tie of an obvious religious significance which is doomed, namely the eating of human livers. In olden times the Gonja peopled used to devour the livers of their vanquished enemies in the belief that the liver is the seat of the spirit. Since the arrival of the British however, human livers have been unprocurable. Nevertheless in Bole at the Festival of New Yams, "Essence of Human Livers" is mixed in the common food pot used by fully grown men. No one is supposed to lift the new yams from his farm until this Festival has been performed, the divisional Chief has eaten some of the new crop and given leave for harvesting to begin.

Den is the great annual Festival of the Nyamase of Western Gonja and is performed at Senyon in honour of the Senyon Kipo Fetish. It takes place about three months before Damba and lasts for three days.

On the first day parties from the surrounding villages converge on Senyon, and in the evening having formed up in file, march into Senyon from different directions to the music of horn and drum. The Seripe people only are not allowed to enter Senyon until the following day though the young men come in by stealth to join the dancing that takes place that night.

At daybreak next day Kibiriwura (the Fetish Priest) climbs to the roof of his house where, seated on an Ashanti Gold Chair and surrounded by other paraphernalia given by devotees from Ashanti, he receives gifts for sacrifice to the Fetish and is greeted by the worshippers. He is accorded the greatest respect; even the Gonja Chiefs who are present salute him with full ceremonial. After a while, he descends and, sitting with the Kupos of the neighbouring villages beneath the three buck horns, and the iron rings that are stuck in the wall of this house, he sacrifices some fowls. Later he again goes up to his roof top.

At about 9 o'clock two horn blowers mount the roof of the Kiniri-wura's house and summon the people to arm and meet for the hunt. Two messengers bearing wooden clubs and a third carrying a wooden sword spotted with red and white and black are sent to Senyonwura and the other Gonja Chiefs who are waiting in the Gonja section of the town to invite them to the hunt. The Kibiriwura descends, and with his Kupo and the Kupos of the other villages he proceeds in file to a tree about three hundred yards outside the village in the direction of Grupe. The Gonjas proceed to a tree opposite and the hunting party gathers with drums beating and horns playing under another tree further away where they pause. The entire male population of the village is now outside, for no man or boy may remain in the village under pain of flogging. Now the hunting party moves to a tree on the Southern side of the village and pauses again. The drums and horns are sent back by small boys to the Kibiriwura and the hunt begins. It continues until a kill has been made, when the hunters collect again near the Kibiriwura. The three processions form and return proceeded by Kibiriwura to the village. Kibiriwura goes to sit with his elders beneath his tree until the Gonja Chiefs have passed to the Senyonwura's section. The Gonjas greet Senyonwura and disperse. Kibiriwura climbs his room into his house. At noon there is drinking and feasting and in the evening the youngsters gather under a tree to the South of the town to dance.

On the third day before dawn Kibiriwura and his Kupo go alone to visit the water-hole and return to the village at daybreak. Save for the presentation and killing of the sacrifices the Festival is ended and the visitors depart. When they have gone Kibiriwura's womenfolk cook the meat from the hunt. Kibiriwura's head is shaved and new farming may begin.

Oaths here, as in the other parts of the Gold Coast, may be sworn on the Paramount Chief, Divisional Chief, a sub-Chief or on the mother of any of these. In certain divisions other oaths may be sworn, usually on some day well remembered in local history. Thus in Bole the terrible Jentilipe oath may be sworn on "The Day of Jentilipe when we fought Samori" and when incidentally the Gonjas suffered a costly defeat. In Debre there is the "Laraba" Oath sworn on "The day when many Chiefs and young men were killed in a fight for the Debre Skin"; and in Tuluwe there is the Alhamisi Oath which combines an oath sworn on the Chief's father with one on a Chief who was killed on a Thursday. Of all the Divisions of Gonja, Kawlaw probably has the two most interesting oaths. They are Agbulung (a slave's neck chain) and Ewurafiase (a slave's leg irons). These oaths originated at a time when Kawlawura was defeated by the Ashantis. He was captured at Kpembe and mistaken for a slave. Later, however, he was recognised and set free. Hence this unique variation of the Divisional Chief's oath.

In the Kpembe Division there is a day of rest every six days which is known as Kulupi. It takes its name from Kulupi village where Ndewura Jakpa rested after his conquest of the Weilas or Abrumasi and the killing of the venomous snake Yaji which inhabited the bank of the Volta River near the town of Yeji which had not then been founded.

GONJA POLITICAL SYSTEM

The Gonja people are ruled by Chiefs of the Royal line of Ndewura Jakpa and his sons. This Chiefship is one over people rather than over land which is still very much the practical concern of the Nyamases. Every scion of this line may aspire to the Paramount Chiefship of Yabum, but he must first be content with a junior Chieftaincy in his Division, which may be a title without a village or if a village, he and his family may well find that they are the only Gonjas there; for the Gonjas are a tiny ruling minority in amongst the more numerous Nyamase. In the olden days there was often a decided reluctance on the part of Gonja Chieftains to leave the seats of the Divisional Chiefs, which are the centres of Gonja culture, and go to live in their bush villages. The court has always exercised its lure for the plotter, the place seeker and pleasure lover. Having obtained his Chieftaincy, he may ascend through the prescribed "gates" to become the Chief of the Division which itself is the final "gate" through which he must pass to Yabum. The process of rising is apt to be a slow one because it involves stepping into dead men's shoes, but the element of luck is always there and a man may become a senior Chief at a relatively early age. Each of the ranks of Gonja commonalty and Chiefship has a name. There are the courtesy titles Napuna (warrior), Cherega ("The Hon."), Lorgna usually given to Ewurichibis in Western Gonja and the Chiefly degrees of Gariba, Yeramu and Wuripe. Of these last all Chieftains are Gariba and to Yabumwura his Divisional Chiefs are also Gariba. Yeramu is a courtesy title for important Chiefs in a Division, but is more strictly reserved to the Divisional Chiefs themselves. Wuripe is the highest title of all which I have only heard used to describe Yabumwura or Kpembewura. When Yabumwura is present he alone is Yeramu or Wuripe.

Naturally, there are variations to this general scheme of things. There is, for instance, the institution of the Ewurichibi Chiefships as opposed to the Ewuribi Chiefships which have been described above. These Chiefships are the perquisites of the male issue of marriages between Gonja Princesses and either non-Gonja Moslem or Nyamase men, but the occupants of these Chiefships are not in the strict way of things eligible for Ewuribi skins.

There are again certain Chieftaincies that descend from father to son and are out of the general scheme of succession to Yabum, just as there are some others which are the reward of a miniature gate system of their own. But the working of the whole system will be seen when the Constitution of Gonja is examined in detail.

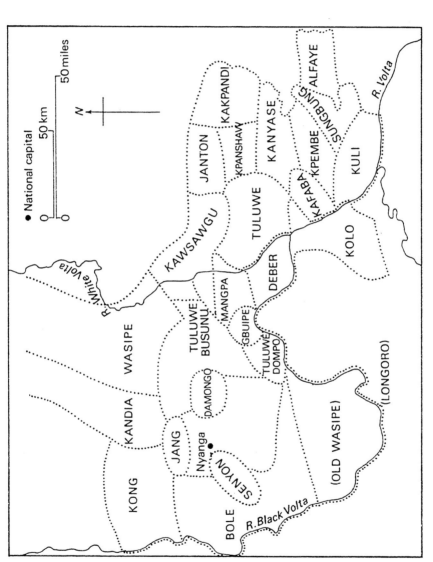

Map 2. Major Territorial divisions of Gonja.

Every Chief of whatever his rank, provided he has a village and is not merely the Chief of an extinct town, has his elders and advisers, the most important of whom will be the Chief of the Nyamase of the village and, if there are Moslems, their Liman. His little Court is the miniature of the Court of the Divisional Chief who will have his Nsawura and Dogtes (heralds), Mbongwura (leader in war), archer, ferrymen (if his lands include a river), drummers, master of horse, sword bearers and horn blowers, Bisepu the guardian of the ancestral walking sticks and Begbangpo (singular Mbangpo) or traditional advisers. Every person has access to him in a system which at its best is a constitutional monarchy of which the monarch is the Divisional Chief and not the remote and frequently ineffectual imperial head.

The Divisional Chiefs are nine in number, all of whom with the exception of Buipe, Kandia and Kong may become Yabumwura. Buipe has never been eligible for the succession.

Kandia was an old Division which extended over a great part of the present Wala District as far even as Walembele, and including Chasie and Ducie, but long ago Kandiawura Jewu renounced his rights to succeed to the Yabum skins.

Kong was a Division that included villages in North Western Gonja and Southern Wala, but its rights of succession to Yabum were withdrawn following the perfidious action of Abudulai Kongwura, nicknamed Kabondogodam, in invoking the aid of Samori to further his claims to the Yabum skins, having already usurped the Kong skins from Nantachi the rightful and rival claimant.

Only with the accession of the present Yabumwura did Wasipewura become eligible for succession to the Yabum skins. Even then it was only offered to him in desperation following the refusal of Kpembe and Bole and because the two previous Yabumwaras from Kusawgu and Tuluwe had each reigned for only a short time.

The nine Divisional Chiefs of which five only are now Gates to the Paramountcy are: Yabum, Buipe, Kpembe, Tuluwe, Bole, Kusawgu, Wasipe, Kong, and Kandia.

YABUM

The name Yabum is said to derive from the words Ya and Bum meaning "Great Company." Besides being the paramount skin it is a Division in the same way as the others. This paramountcy must have been very shadowy before the coming of the Europeans, for Divisional Chiefs were neither eager to claim it when it fell vacant nor did they accord its occupant any significant respect. Indeed Captain Nash's remark in 1907 that the Yabumwura's authority extended only over the Bole area would seem to emphasise its shadowy nature.

The succession to the skin is through the Gates of Kpembe, Tuluwe, Bole, Kusawgu and now Wasipe. There is an ancient Kapok tree at Nyanga whose buttress roots each represent one of the Gates to the paramountcy. On the appropriate buttress, notches are cut to represent the Yabumwuras who have come from that Gate. So far there is no buttress representing the Wasipe Gate.

When a Yabumwura dies and until the appointment of his successor, Senyonwura acts as Regent and custodian of the skin property. His is the effective power though the late Yabumwura's eldest son and eldest daughter who are called Ewurakung, are given white robes and sit traditionally in their father's stead. Senyonwura sends the late Chief's horse and sandals to Buipewura as proof of his decease. The Divisional Chiefs then meet to choose a successor from amongst their number and when this is done they ask Senyonwura to send a messenger to Buipewura giving him the name of their nominee which he automatically approves.

The Kagbapewura, a Nyamase and a Chief of the Buipe Division, then comes to enrobe the Yabumwura elect. This ceremony is performed at a place in the bush about one kilometre South of Nyanga the traditional capital of Gonja—the capital was moved to Damongo in 1944—and no Gonja is allowed to witness it though they may await the coming of their newly enrobed Paramount Chief a little way off. Having performed the ceremony Kagbapewura turns away and starts his return journey to Buipe for neither he nor Buipewura may ever see Yabumwura again. Yabumwura is hedged about with other taboos. He may not see the Yabumwuras' burial place at Mankuma so when he has to go through that village he covers his head. He may not walk about in Bole. When he visits there he stays in his village of Chorobang less than a mile away. His mother may not live in Nyanga with him because a son must act on the advice of his mother and father and that would be unseemly for a Paramount Chief to be thus obliged to accept a subject's advice. Nor may he or any Divisional Chief eat elephant which are the princes of the bush animals as such would be regarded as a sort of cannibalism. He used never to leave Nyanga or to cross the White Volta River, but both these taboos have now been broken.

When the British first came to the Northern Territories they believed Kpembewura ("the King of Kombi") to be the Paramount Chief of the Gonjas. They may have been lead into error because for some time Yabum had been a perquisite of the Bole gate and naturally the Eastern Divisions, who tacitly agreed that Kpembewura was their senior, were not going to disabuse them, and consequently became subjects of the Western Gonjas. This state of affairs came about when Wari Pereku (Wari the Stout) from Kusawgu was Yabumwura. He had not been at Nyanga for long when he was defeated at Jentilipe by the Bole people under Amadu Jaga (Red Bull), with whom he had been constantly at loggerheads. This decided him to return to his native Kusawgu, which he never reached because he died on the way thither at Supuni where he was buried. On account of Wari Pereku's experience the Eastern Chiefs, Tuluwewura and Kusawguwura decided not to take the Yabum skins in future and to recognise Kpembewura as their superior. Only in the 1930s after the Yapei conference did they take up their claims to Yabum again. Even then they were unlucky, for on the death of Yabumwura Mam (Bole), first a Tuluwewura, then a Kusawguwura succeeded, but neither lived for more than a short time. Kusawguwura did not wish to succeed and was anxious all the way to Nyanga. At Supuni he sacrificed fowls in honour of Wari Pereku but that brought little comfort for he felt his approaching doom. He was however, during his short reign to have Wari Pereku's body exhumed and buried at Mankuma with other dead Yabumwuras.

Though the Yabumwura is the Paramount Chief of Gonja there is an office that is higher than his. It is the office of Buruwura which can be achieved only by a reigning Yabumwura. The title probably derives from the Gonja word "Buru" which means "Weak" or "Broken," and a Yabum-wura becomes Buruwura when age and infirmity render him incapable of effective rule. Then he lives at Nyanga, is assisted in every act and is not even allowed to move by himself. Thus originated the saying "When Buruwura turned the whole of Gonja turned," for when the old man moved, his followers moved also so that they would be able to see his face. When a Yabumwura became Buruwura his son dealt with affairs of state until the Buruwura died when a new Yabumwura would be chosen in the normal way.

So far as can be ascertained, there have been only two Buruwuras. The first was Lanyon who was one of the very early Yabumwuras and the other was Bori from Kpembe. It is probable that Bori was compara-tively young when he was forced into the office of Buruwura. At any rate his resentment at this treatment gave him strength to escape to Kpembe with the Buru skin and traditional trappings. He died there. During the time of Kpembewura Isanurafu, one Chakpatasi came to Kpembe and caused a riot as a diversion while he attempted to recover the Buru property. He was only partly successful as the skin itself was destroyed and some of the other property remained in Kpembe. Bori's treatment is said to be the cause of Kpembe's alienation from Yabumwura and his vaunted independence of him.

The distinction between Yabumwura's functions as a Paramount Chief and as a Divisional Chief is shown by the fact that he has two sets of Begbangpo or elders.

The Paramount set which advise him on matters affecting the State as a whole, such as land and Chiefship disputes are, Senyonwura, Damongowura, Debrewura, Mongpawura, Kawlawura and Choriwura.

There is some confusion about the origin of their special privileges which are the establishment of their villages as sanctuaries, the exemption from sending tribute to Yabumwura, and the celebration of Damba in their own villages. All of them claim that they once had the right of succession as Divisional Chiefs to the Yabum skins which they renounced in favour of "the Chiefs of our younger brothers" and were given instead the privileges they now enjoy. Their peculiar position is emphasised in that all Divisional Chiefs pay them the respect of removing their hats and sandals when greeting them.

The State Begbangpo

The *Senyon* family traces its descent from Lanyon, son of Ndewura Jakpa who renounced his rights of succession to Yabum. When a Senyonwura dies Yabumwura is notified and he asks the family to choose the heir, which is done according to the normal rules of succession in Gonja. The successor is then enrobed by the Dakrupe Liman.

The *Damongo* family traces its descent from Gbinnynti "Too Tired," a younger brother of Lanyon Senyonwura. Lanyon became Yabumwura but finding he much preferred his previous position renounced his right of succession and advised his younger brother to do so also. These Chiefs are chosen and enrobed by Kutunkuruwura (the Chieftain of the Drums), so called because he is the guardian of the Kutunkuru drum given by Ndewura Jakpa to his son. Damongowura is also the owner of an Mbon-tikuribi or "Stomach Drum" which legend says was found in the stomach of an elephant.

Debrewura is chosen by Opungiwura the Fetish Priest of Kpansera who may not himself succeed, from three gate families Bumbum, Kapoasi and Abrasi which follow one another in rotation. The Debrewura stays in his gate village as there is no actual village of Debre. The first Debrewura was Kongkange, son of "the Second Jakpa" (according to District Records) and grandson of Kodiwura whose place it was. At one time until about 1945 Debrewura followed Buipe and used to perform Buipewura's funeral customs.

Mangpawura succeeds through two gates. He claims that when asked to go to Yabum an ancient Mangpawura declined and gave the chance to his younger brother Tuluwe as he preferred to remain in Butie. He used to give tribute to Debrewura his elder brother, like whom he followed Buipe.

Butie is unique in Gonja. It was founded by Mpara people who were driven from Longoro by Ashanti invaders and settled in Jembito where they were absorbed in Jakpa's host. Eventually they settled in Butie where they built the famous two and three storey mud fortresses which defeated every attempt of the Ashantis to overwhelm them. So bitter was the Mpara feud with the Ashantis that they swore never to allow the Ashantis to visit Butie again. The Ashantis swore a complementary oath. If an Ashanti came to town after that his arms and legs were broken and he was dropped alive into one of the numerous wells, which the Mpara had bored through the rock in this neighbourhood and, which was subsequently sealed with a stone. The fortresses were rectangular in shape and consisted of two or three rooms built one on top of the other. They were built on mounds some ten feet high in this way. First a basement room was dug into the mound and roofed with wooden rafters and swish in the usual Western Gonja fashion. The roofs of the lower rooms formed the floors of the upper, and the first and second stories rose above the mound. The upper stories covered the same area as the basement, which was used to accommodate livestock and in the dry weather the flat roof of the "fortress" was used for sleeping. When intact these buildings probably rose to a height of some 30 ft. To support the structure it seems some of the walls were chosen as bearer walls and built of double thickness. These fortresses of which there were six are now mere ruins and there were others in Berang or Bara. Naturally Butie was a sanctuary for runaway slaves and a forward base for war against Ashanti.

Kawlawwura comes from three families each of which has a gate skin. The head of the Jawupe family is Kabasiwura who lives at Tarapa (Kagbatata), that of the Chapegi family is Chapowura who lives at Siriminchu and that of Kabiapi is Kebiawura who lives at Kajau. Neither Chepowura nor Kebiawura need hold any previous Chieftaincy, but Kabasiwura must succeed to his skin through the Cherimbu gate. A new Kawlawwura must be approved by the Brumasiwura and the Bolasipiwura with their elders before his name is conveyed to the Yabumwura. The Mbonwura of Kawlaw lives at Kabako.

Choriwuras succeed through a gate system of which the Chieftaincy of Kanyangbon is one of the gates. Jang is the Choriwura's village.

The Divisional Begbangpo of Yabum are Kakulasiwura, Sakpawura, Biawura and Tariwura.

Kakulasiwura ("the Whisperer") sat beside Yabumwura telling him what was happening in the Division. Sakpawura when Damba drew near went round the villages telling the people of the Festival's approach and collecting from them presents for the Yabumwura. He was the Keeper of the Yabumwura's eunuchs (kitibi), though probably not a eunuch himself. These young boys, who had been sent by the Divisional chiefs as harem attendants, he castrated and trained at Balepi (Not Men's Town, Vagella). The boys were not necessarily Gonjas. He also schooled Yabumwura's sons in the duties of Chiefship, etc., and was Yabumwura's legal expert. The eunuchs were a privileged class who were not punished for theft. Biawura took the lead in war. Tariwura's special function is not recorded.

Both Sakpawura and Biawura have the privilege of taking what they want of the presents given to the Yabumwura. These Divisional Mbangpo have direct access to the Yabumwura and unlike the State Mbangpo are neither accorded nor give any particular marks of respect to other Chiefs. Other persons had to approach the Yabumwura through one of these Mbangpo.

Succession to the Chieftaincies of Kakulasi, Bia and Tari is by the choice of Yabumwura's Dogte amongst those eligible for each of them. Senyonwura, however, always chooses the Sakpawura.

Of the Yabum villages some have interesting histories. Fumbo for instance is peopled by the descendants of Dagomba mercenaries from Jambaraga or Benge, employed by Tuluwewura Jewu in his bid to seize the Yabum skin by force. They were first rewarded for their services by being allowed to settle under Duatsukuru at Dua. While there they intermarried with the Mos and adopted their title of Koro and their language, which is spoken in Fumbo to this day. From Dua they moved to Lambo (now in ruins) where they were harassed by the Nkoranzas. Their Chief, Koro Berenge, therefore went to Yabumwura Jakpa who gave them land at Fumbo where they have since remained. Until Tuluwewura was defeated by Samori at Jentilipe the Fumbo people used to dance Damba in that village. Then there are the Moslem villages of Larabanga and Dokurupe whose Mara speaking people came in the same migratory wave. The inhabitants of Kananto, Kabampe and Kabalima also make the interesting claim that they were some of the original followers of Yabumwura from Beawu (see Appendix XI).

Buipe Division

The Buipewura ranks next to Yabumwura in the Gonja hierarchy. Some give him a position almost equal to that of the Paramount Chief. This pre-eminence amongst Divisional Chiefs has been attributed to various causes amongst which are these; that he and Yabumwura were descended from twins who contested the succession to the Paramountcy and were never subsequently allowed to see one another; that he is not a Divisional Chief at all, but merely a very potent Priest who derives his authority from being the guardian of Ndewura Jakpa's tomb. The first version may be due to a confusion with the origin of the Buipe gate system, the second is that held by most of the Gonjas outside Buipe who further claim that Buipewura's ancestors were merely followers of Ndewura Jakpa and not his sons. Kpembewura claimed never to have heard of Ewurakpur and was quite definite that Wari Kaluwi of Kusawgu was the Ndewura's youngest son. This is the story of the foundation of the Divisional System and of the origin of Buipewura's peculiar position as expounded by Buipewura, Buipe Liman and their elders in 1953.

When Ndewura Jakpa came to Buipe he found the place in the charge of the Nyamase Chief Kanyampasewura. He liked it, built a house there and left Buipe with other villages in the hands of Ewurakpur, (Ewurakpur means Chief's House in Gonja), his youngest and favourite son, to rule while he was at the wars. For in those days Buipe was the great kola market between North and South. During his campaign against the Ashantis Ndewura Jakpa who, according to the Buipe tradition was an old man, fell sick at Brumasi and fearing death told his people to take him to Buipe. He was carried thither by his Royal relatives, died there in Ewurakpur's arms and was buried. The version favoured by the other Divisions is that Ndewura Jakpa was in full vigour at Brumasi where he was killed in battle with the Ashantis. He cried "Abrumasi" (I am killed). His people tried to carry his body to Nyanga for burial, but it began to decompose on the way and so after all they decided to bury it at Buipe. Ewurakpur, who now sat in his father's place, sent messengers to summon the other sons of Ndewura Jakpa to Buipe. They came and all save the eldest greeted him by removing their caps in the traditional manner. Ewurakpur asked the eldest why he alone had not greeted him as the others. He replied "Because I am my father's eldest son and you are my younger brother." To which Ewurakpur retorted "Then I shall not doff my cap to you either." Now it happened that before he died, Ndewura Jakpa had said that of all of his children only Ewurakpur was empowered to confer Chiefship. So Ndewura Jakpa's eldest son went to his house to think over developments and when his ire had cooled he emerged to ask pardon of Ewurakpur who afterwards enrobed him Yabumwura, Paramount Chief of the Gonjas. Ewurakpur then enrobed Ndewura Jakpa's other sons as Divisional Chiefs. Since that day it has been forbidden for a Yabumwura and a Buipewura to meet, because a senior son had found his youngest brother sitting in his father's place, and if they were to meet one of them would surely die. Now Buipewura, through one of his sub-Chiefs, enrobes only Yabumwura, though in early days he claims to have enrobed Tuluwewura and Kusawguwura also.

Besides being guardian of Ndewura Jakpa's tomb, Buipewura was also the peacemaker between warring Chiefs. When he heard that war was about to break out between two Chiefs he sent to the aggressor to counsel moderation and if that failed he tried to mediate between the parties. It was believed that bad luck would dog any man who refused his mediation.

The two gate families to the Buipe skin are descended from twin sons. One of them became Buipewura, while his brother who succeeded him first of all became Kakpandewura. These families are respectively the Denkeripibi who succeed through either the Gbunbunsu skin or the Danyapi skin and the Labopibi who succeed through the Silima skin. A dying Buipewura indicates his successor by pointing at him with his stick, but in fact, this choice is limited to the head of the house whose turn for succession it is.

As his elders, Buipewura has of course his Liman, and besides him, Kanyampasewura of the Nyinipe family the head of the local Dagombas, Japewura, the Chief of Kalonso, Boakipewura, Mantowura and Kanton-wura the Chief of Fryfusu. The senior Ewuriche of the Division is Mantowuriche.

The Nyamase of Buipe are Dagomba and Dompo people. We have seen that Kanyampasewura is the Tindaana and head of the former. Of the latter, Dompowura who lives at Jembito is Chief. These Dompos, who are said to speak a language which may be similar to that of the Butie people, but it has been impossible to check this as Mpara is no longer spoken, came from Longoro before the Mos settled in that place and originally put themselves under the protection of the Tuluwewura. They may share with the Butie people a common Brong origin as they have the tradition of originating from a hole in the ground and the custom of killing the seventh child.

Kpembe Division

The Kpembe Division differs from the others in that the three gate Chiefs each have villages under them. So indeed do some of the other senior Chiefs of the Division, who however are not in the line for the Kpembe skin, namely Panshiaw, Janton, Kakpande, Kafaba and Kilibi. The gate Chiefs are Sumbungwura, head of the Sumbung family, Kanakulaiwura of Alfai, head of the Lepo family, and Kanyasiwura, head of the Kanyasi family, who are all descended from Ndewura Jakpa's second son. In olden times the Sumbung and Lepo families kept the succession to Kpembe to themselves and excluded the Kanyasi family which had an equally good claim. In 1894 however, the Kanyasi family led by Kabache-wura revolted and with Dagomba help deposed Kpembewura Napo, defeated the forces of Sumbung and Lepo and sacked Salaga. Sumbung-wura Lanto was amongst the Chiefs killed in the battle, and many of the survivors fled across the Daka River to Bagjamso, to Alfai and to Krachi. Kabachewura then summoned Kanyasiwura, his elder brother, who was enrobed as Kpembewura. Later the senior fugitive of the Sumbung family returned from Krachi and was enrobed Sumbungwura. The Germans, however, would not allow Kanakulaiwura to return. After the war a council was held at Papitia (now in ruins) and an oath was taken to do away with wars of succession in the future. Henceforth it was agreed that the houses of Sumbung, Lepo and Kanyasi should succeed to Kpembe in turn. This, however, seems to have been a dead letter for the next three Chiefs came from the Kanyasi gate until Soale, the first Sumbung to succeed for a century came on. The present Chief comes from the Kanyasi gate once more.

Kpembewuras are appointed in this way. When the funeral celebrations of the dead Chief have been completed, all the Gonjas are summoned to assemble in an open space near the Kpembe dam. First of all there is an open discussion. Then the "Electors"—Kilibiwura of Kuli, Kafabawura, Kawasiwura, the Kanyamase Jankwasiwura of Kulupi who is responsible for the burial of Kpembewura but whose office has been vacant since about 1936, Kpembe Liman, Lamporwura, and Salagawura who was appointed by the British as the late Lamporwura whose successor has not yet been chosen, was considered too feeble to serve—go apart to deliberate. Normally this is a purely formal affair, but in the event of a dispute over the succession, which will anyhow be only within the family whose turn it is to succeed, the Liman counsels patience and the discussion is thrown open. When the Electors have finished they return to the open space and call the Ewuribi to bring their senior forth. They then announce their choice which is in the normal course of events already known, tell the chief elect that he will be enrobed on a day to be named by the Liman, and Kafabawura relates to the multitude how Ndewura Jakpa made him a peacemaker. The Chief elect gives each of them a small present, then all disperse to await the Liman's choice of a propitious day. On the day before his enrobement, Mljikowura, as the Chief elect is now called, is taken into a secret room by Kawasiwura, Nakpaiwura and Mabonwura to see the skin properties, which no other person entitled to the Kpembe skin may see.

On the chosen day all meet in the same place and the Chief elect is brought from his house by the Liman, the Niami and Kunkwawura. He brings with him a white cap, a white gown and white trousers and sits down in a clearing in the centre of the crowd. The clothes are put in a basket and taken round for each Chief to see. Next each of the Enume Ping Bupo, or elders responsible for the enrobement, namely Jankwasiwura, the Liman (White Robe) and the Nsawura (White Cap for he only is allowed to touch a Chief's head), takes the garment for which he is responsible and helps the Chief to put it on. Sandals are placed before him and Kawasiwura guides his feet into them. Then a white cow is brought and slaughtered in front of the Chief whom the Enumu Ping Bupo help to step over it. A hoe, a knife, a bow and arrow are put before him and he is asked to make his choice between them. If he chooses the hoe his reign will be peaceful and prosperous, if the knife it will be scarred by the wounds of internal strife, and if the bow and arrow he will have war. Every Chief nowadays chooses the hoe, the symbol of peace. When this is done the young men of the new Chief's family bring him a bridled but unsaddled horse which he rides in procession to his house to the beating of drums and the firing of guns; and thus ends the ceremony. After the enrobement the guardians of the skin property give Kpembewura one of the sticks of his predecessors which he will use throughout his reign. He remains in his house for seven days when he emerges in all his finery to tell the people his policy and his ideas on governance.

The enrobement of junior Chiefs follows a similar pattern and is the same in all Divisions. Seven days before the event the candidate collects food and tells his women to prepare it and to make pito (the local beer). He also sends a gift of kola nuts to the village of which he has been appointed Chief, and if the villagers accept the gift all is well. If they return it, however, it means that they do not want the donor as their Chief on any account. On the day of his enrobement he retires and strips himself of all his clothes save a new pair of white trousers. Thus clad he goes before Kpembewura in the Chief's house. Kpembewura asks him:

> If I call you in the day time will you come?
> If I call you in the night time will you come?
> If I have work to do will you help me?

To which the candidate replies "I will."

He is then enrobed in a white robe, and given a white cap, sandals and a staff. After this he retires to his compound where he remains for seven days. He distributes food, pito and money and everyone who wishes feasts and dances at his expense. During his seven days retreat the new Chief continues to wear his white habit. On the seventh day he emerges clad in rich clothes and goes to greet Kpembewura. Henceforth he assumes the ordinary duties of a Chief.

In this place it may not be inappropriate to mention one of the taboos that attach to Divisional Chiefs. They may not farm because they are kept in food by their subjects. Should they wish to make a farm of their own, however, they always have a labour force ready, for all twins and "Red Children" are given to them.

The appointment of Sumbungwura, Kanyasiwura and Kanakulaiwura operates through the gate system. Two families, Laba and Sumbung are eligible for the Sumbung skin, to which they succeed alternately through the Chieftaincies of Sangule, Sangkung, Kuntungda and Lambung. The Kanyasi family is divided into two parts sprung from a common ancestor. They are called Kaputibunto and Kaputibito and succession to the Kanyasi skin is confined to their members. Kabache is normally the gate for Kanyasi and Bambale the gate for Kabache.

In Alfai succession to the Kanakulai skin alternates between the Kujolobitobi and the Jawullapibi branches of the Lepo family, which traces its descent from Djolo, grandson of Ndewura Jakpa and known as the Spearer of Hippopotamus Meat. Succession is through the Dusai gate.

A Kanakulaiwura may nominate his successor from his own family or if he dies without doing so the elders choose the new Chief. The new Chief is taken to Kpembe for the approval of Kpembewura and is enrobed either at Kpembe or on his return to Kpandai. He goes into his house and vests himself in his Chief's robes. Having done so he comes out and in front of the assembled people draws his sword which he points first to the sky and then to the ground, to show that he is responsible to God for the land. The origin of this custom of self enrobement occurred on the death of Jakpa while fighting the Konkombas between Kabri and Samuri. When they heard of their leader's death the Gonjas wanted to flee, but Kanakulaiwura his son, went into the house and put on all Jakpa's robes and ornaments. When he came out and sat on the lion skin and cushion the people said "Behold, there is Jakpa" and took new heart. This too is the reason Kanakulaiwura sits on lion or leopard skins and not on kob skins like Sumbungwura or Kanyasiwura.

During his reign Kanakulaiwura is subject to various taboos. He may not tell lies, take bribes or steal another man's wife. He may not walk barefoot in the bush or on his farm and he may not hunt. He may not flog a person though he may point at him with his Mallam's stick. He may farm. Between the death of one Kanakulaiwura and the enrobement of another, the ceremonial lion and leopard skins, the cushion and other skin property are looked after by an important elder called Kunkwawura.

The Begbangpo of the Division

The appointment of Lepowura is one that has been misunderstood in the past. He is an Mbagpo of Kpembewura's and nothing more. The office is not hereditary, but is given by a Kpembewura to one of his gatesmen and when a new Kpembewura succeeds from another gate the old Lepo may be dismissed and a new one appointed. Lepowura helps Kawasi-wura in his duties as Chamberlain. His particular responsibility is collecting the food gifts from the butchers of Salaga and conveying them to Kpembewura's soup pot. The office is said to take its name from one Lepo who was left in charge of the Kpembe Division while a certain Kpembewura took his army to try, unsuccessfully, to take the Yabum skins by force.

Kawasiwura is the guardian of the skin property in the interval between the death of one Kpembewura and the enrobement of another, or in his absence the duty is done by Kilibiwura, Kafabawura or Jankwasiwura. He is also the first in any assembly to greet Kpembewura and in the old days it was his duty to see the Chief at cock crow and to accompany any early morning visitor.

Kilibiwura is a very important elder. So much so that he is often given the title "Yeramu" even in Kpembewura's presence. His village is

Juli but he now lives at Makongo in order to be on the main road. The gate Chieftaincy to Kilibi is that of Mangopangwura Chief of Makongo but this custom is of recent origin. Kilibiwura dances Damba in his own village.

Kafabawura also had special duties. In times of war he would come to Kpembe to pray for victory. He did not engage in war himself for when he was met at Siriminchu (or Kotokunji) by the Moslems of a village on the opposite bank of the river with that mixture of water and grain which is called "Kafa," Ndewura Jakpa declared that in future their village would be called Kafaba, and made it a sanctuary and its Chief a peacemaker. He is also a mediator between a Chieftain who may have done wrong and his Chief. The Dagombas refer to him as their grandfather. In this office Kafabawura's powers are similar to those of Buipewura. The succession to the Kafaba skin is in one family and follows the usual Gonja inheritance pattern. Kafabawura has no rights of succession to Kpembe. He dances Damba in his own village.

Korasiwura, a Gonja Chief of Kulupi village was also an important elder but the post like that of Jankwasiwura, also of Kulupi, has been vacant for some years.

The Mparaba Sub-Divisions of Kpembe

There are three Mparaba Sub-Divisions, Panshiaw, Janton and Kakpande of which Panshiaw is the senior. Each of these includes many villages and the Janton and Kakpande groups owe allegiance through their Chiefs to Panshiawwura though neither Jantonwura nor Kakpandewura succeeds to the Panashiaw skin. One early Panshiawwura called Adama succeeded from Kakpande however. In their dealings with Kpembewura, Panshiawwura and Jantonwura go through Sumbungwura while Kakpandewura serves Kpembewura through Kanyasewura. All three Chiefs dance Damba in their own villages.

When the Panshiaw skin falls vacant Numwura succeeds, for there is only the one gate here. The Jantonwura and the Kakpandewura, however, are formally consulted about the succession and invariably acknowledge the new Chief. Kawkawyiri-enum is Mbonwura of Panshiaw.

In both Janton and Kakpande Sub-Divisions succession to the Chiefship is through a gate system. In Janton there are two gate families which bear the names Chetulapibi and Bamvimpibi and succeed through the Chieftaincies of Chetula and Bamvim respectively. The Janton Chieftaincy of Byta or Puja is reserved for Ewurechibis who, of course, may not become Jantonwura.

In Kakpande the Jupebi family succeed through the Nienseli and Pallie skins while the Bupabi family go through Nymalaga. It is interesting to note that Ndewura Jakpa gave Kakpandewura one of the Sakparebi Limans. Kakpandewura explained this as perhaps being due to his people's relationship with the people of Buipe.

To depart from the theme of this essay for a moment. The Mparaba people were early associated with the British for in 1902 when Captain Armitage was planning to visit Savelugu from Tamale, it was Soale Jantonwura who saved his life by warning him of a Dagomba plot to assassinate him. He foiled the plot by going to Daboya instead.

Salaga itself is a place of interest. Originally a Nanumba village under the Suzerainty of Bimbilla Na, it was conquered by Ndewura Jakpa who, however, let the Chiefship remain in the reigning Nanumba family which was the arrangement until 1933 when Kpembewura gave the skin to a Gonja at the same time confirming the old Nanumba family as Tindaanas of Salaga. After its conquest by the Gonjas, Salaga began to attract Hausa settlers and quickly grew into an important Moslem market town eclipsing the old kola markets of Buipe and Mpaba. The Hausas did not extend their trading activities South of the Volta River because the Ashantis were interested in no commodity except slaves. Salaga however became a big slave market at this time and the slaves were bought and sold under the large tree that still stands in the market place. The price of a good slave was about £10. The traffic however received its death blow in 1874 with the defeat of Kofi Karikari the Asantehene and the abolition of slavery in the Colony. Under the same "slave" tree in the market place the tribute from Kpembe was paid to the Asantehene's representative.

Wasipe Division

The Wasipe family is descended from Denyan the third son of Ndewura Jakpa who was the twin of the first Kpembewura. Since that time in any assembly of the Chiefs of Gonja, Kpembewura and Wasipewura go together to greet Yabumwura followed by the other Divisional Chiefs in their order of seniority.

The Wasipe Division came into Gonja hands in an extraordinary way. The Tampluma Chief of the area who was called Jangbologuwura was being harassed by the Dagombas and fearing defeat sent to Denyan the Chief of the small village of Wasipe, South of Bole, to come to his aid with his people. Denyan Wasipewura came, and due to his help the Dagombas were defeated. He settled in the Kawasi section of Daboya and his son settled in the Tarima section of the town. He soon found that there was salt on the river bank near the town and sent some to Yabumwura who distributed it amongst his people. They marvelled and said "Nda Peye bo Anyia," "Our brother's land is better than our's" which has been shortened to form the name Daboya. Meanwhile Jangbologuwura was so grateful for his deliverance that he honoured his friend by giving him the tribute from Daboya Market and when Damba came round danced Damba before him. This was the thin end of the wedge for Jang-bologuwura's son Adu, whose attempt to celebrate Damba separately and to claim back the market tribute which his father in his enthusiasm had given to Denyan, met with a rebuttal from Denyan's son who would have none of it. Jangbologuwura however, retains the privilege of enrobing the Wasipewura, but the skin is now vacant and the one known descendant is on the Coast and cannot be persuaded to return.

As the descendant of a son of Ndewura Jakpa, Wasipewura was originally entitled to succeed to the Paramount skin of Yabum, but the privilege was withdrawn until Ewuntoma, the present Yabumwura, because no other gate wanted the skin, was able to succeed. This is how the ban came about. Once long ago, the Sakparebi family, descendants of Mallam Fatu Morukpe, visited Daboya but were not given the customary entertainment by Wasipewura that is meted out to all strangers. Their surprise at this treatment turned to anger when they saw food being prepared but were given none. So they reported the matter to Yabumwura. A meeting of the Divisional Chiefs was called at which the Sakparebi, as is their custom, placed the skins for the Chiefs to sit on. They took away and destroyed Wasipewura's skin however and his family was thenceforth disqualified from the succession to the Paramountcy.

There are two families which may succeed to Wasipe through the one gate skin of Yarizori. They are the Mamapibi and the Titperipibi. There was a third family, Garimawuripipibi, but it gave only one Divisional Chief long ago and after the death of Wasipewura Mbeima it was excluded from the succession.

Wasipe Nyamase are Tampluma, Anga, and Nwambeli or Black Dagombas. The Anga villages are now only thinly populated because some fifty years ago they supported the Yarizoriwura's usurpation of the Wasipe skins. When three years later having marshalled his forces in Dagomba, the rightful Wasipewura returned to defeat the usurper he punished the Angas and cut of Yarizoriwura's head which is still supposed to be in Daboya to-day. The Tamplumas supported Wasipe-wura.

Daboya is a place that has seen better days. It is on the declining central cattle route fron Navrongo to Kintampo via Buipe. It was an important source of salt for the Northern Territories until the industry, except for local purposes, was killed by the importation of salt from Ada. It is also a centre of cotton growing, spinning, weaving and dyeing—indeed Daboya cloth is famous for its quality throughout Gonja.

Tuluwe or Turugu Division

Tuluwewura's title derives from "Tor-wura" or "Falling Chief" because he came to Tuluwe by surprise. He is descended from Abase Singbing-wura the fourth son of Ndewura Jakpa, for the ancestors of Wasipewura and Kpembewura were twins. Succession alternates between the Jewupe family of Chama and the Kalipe family of Tuluwe which are descended from two brothers who in turn became Tuluwewura. The head of the family which has not supplied the reigning Tuluwewura is elected Bundawura, the title held by the heir apparent. Jallawura and Ehefijiwura choose the new Tuluwewura who used to be enrobed at Buipe until the practice was stopped in 1945. Kpembewura claims that in the old days he was consulted about the appointment to Tuluwe and Kusawgu. If the Tuluwewura is a Kalipe man he lives at Tuluwe and if a Jewupe at Chama, though at one time Benyalipe was the seat of Tuluwewura. Henceforth Tuluwe is likely to be his seat as it is the terminus of a dry season motor road and the Headquarters of the Local Council. During the absence of the Divisional Chief the Dompowura and the Jallowura act on his behalf.

As this is a large Division it is divided into two sections. The Southern one comes directly under Tuluwewura while the Northern one comes under Busumuwura. In the Southern section the land is divided as follows:

Tuluwewura has Chama, Yala, Jitasi, Palangasi and Jakpasolde (Jakpasori).
Bundawura has Dabopi, Nianta and Kaliku (in ruins).
Jallawura has Kachasi and Tuluwe.
Chefigiwura has Nialala.

Jukukuwura and Digmawura have only their own villages and are succeeded by their sons or if they have none by the nominee of Tuluwewura.

The Nyamase of this section belong to three tribes. In the West there are the Dompo under their Chief "Dompowura" who appoints the Kasalewuras of Benyalipe, Boakipe, Kadelso and Bilimpe in Ashanti, Kpajeto in ruins and Morno which used to be in Tuluwe. To become Dompowura a man need have held to previous Chieftaincy. Further East there are the Mpara who live in Jukuku, Kolofu, Tomaklaw, Chama, Nialala, Tuluwe, Kachasi and Kichaleso (ruins). Finally there are the Ntrafo whose territory is East of the Kalurakun River and comprises the villages of Yala, Palangasi, Deba, Jakpasoldi, Kalurakunase and Ksliku (ruins).

There are some interesting places in this section too. Nianta for instance contains several old smelting works which Ndewura Jakpa is reputed to have used. The iron was drawn from the laterite stone of the neighbourhood. Then there is Chama which from a constitutional point of view is of great interest because though there are sections for the Nsogo or Moslems under their Liman, the Gonjas and the Nyamase, the whole is under the rule of Kabiriwura, wealthy Priest of the Lansah Fetish. Chama was probably first an Mpara village under a Kasalewura who still occupies a junior position; then the Nyamase with Kabiriwura came there from Techiman in the train of Ndewura Jakpa's army. Finally a branch of the Tuluwe ruling house with its Moslems moved in from Tuluwe. This together with the liberality of the Fetish Priest might explain the constitutional anomaly of Chama.

Busunu. The origin of Busunuwura's position as ruler of the Northern section and Mbonwura of Tuluwe lies deep in history. Abase, the first Tuluwewura, had a bastard son whom he exiled. When Abase died and was succeeded by his eldest son the new Tuluwewura felt that he must not forsake his exiled half brother. He therefore sent forces to Busunu where his half brother was staying, thus providing him with the means to conquer Busunu and win himself a Chiefship, Busunuwura has no right of succession to the Tuluwe skin however. He is succeeded through a gate system by the Chiefs of Murugu, Supini, Lankatere and Bidima. His rule extends over these villages together with Grupe, Furugu, and Kadindilipe or Barka.

The Nyamase of this section are Anga save in Grupe which was transferred from Senyon as part of a dowry and where the people are Vagella.

Bole Division

Bolewuras are descended from the fifth of Ndewura Jakpa's sons. There are three families in this Division which trace descent from the fifth son of Ndewura Jakpa and from which Bolewuras are chosen. There are also three gate Chiefships which are filled by the heads of each of these families; the Jagapibi, the Safapibi, and the Denkerepibi. The gate skins are Mandare through which a new Bolewura must pass, Jentilipe and Wulasi. The last two gates may not always have been gates to Bole for Buanfo is, or was, the gate to Mandare. Actually, however, the rule has been broken because in 1928 Bolewura Takoro succeeded to the Chiefship from Tuna and even the Ewuribi rule of succession was broken when Bolewura Jubodi (Natorma) an Ewurichibi succeeded from Seripe.

When a Bolewura dies he is buried at Banzini about half a mile South of Bole to the right of the Bamboi road. This is the site of the old Gonja section of Bole, for the present town is sited around the Vagella settlement. It is believed locally that the approaching death of a Bolewura is proclaimed by a column of light which appears above Banzini at night time and is visible only to the Nyamases. The first part of the funeral custom lasts for one month after which the women go into Purdah for eight days and the Yabumwura announces the name of the new Chief. There is a second part of the funeral custom a month later and another after one year. Then each successive year the surviving members of the dead Bolewura's family may, if they are rich enough, sacrifice a cow or something in his honour.

Bolewura's elders are Seripewura, Kajumowura, Kademawura, Mankumawura and the Liman. Of these Kajumowura and Kademawura are Nyamase, and Mankumawura is the guardian of the Yabumwura's burial ground which is situated at Mankuma, but the most important is Seripewura the senior Ewurichibi.

The Ewurichibis and the Ewuriches seem to play a more important part in the affairs of this Division than in any other. The Ewurichibis are the sons or daughters of any Royal Chief's sisters or daughters who have married Nyamase or Moslem men. The sons are entitled in this Division to the skins of Seripe, Kulmasa, Maluwe and Ponponsuri, but may not succeed to that of Bole. Because of this disqualification they were not subject to punishment for any wrongs they might do. Besides this, in the old days if any Chief's son wanted a favour from either Bolewura or Yabumwura he first approached Seripewura. Seripewura is also the adviser to Bolewura who organises such festivals as Damba and accompanies his master wherever he goes but now this last role is confined to important occasions and journeys. He is not an Mbangpo in the ordinary sense for he has none of their peculiar privileges. Seripe became the senior Ewurichibi skin because once, in the time of Yabumwura Awusi, when it became vacant and no one wanted it, the people persuaded Bolewura to make an appointment and he gave it to his sister's son who sacrificed to the Seripe skin. It is said in Bole that the Ewurichibi skins were originally founded as a reward for the services of the Royal women at the battle of Seripe.

Ewuriches are women Chiefs and any Royal Gonja woman who "has become a man" is eligible and may become one after she has approached Bolewura through the dogtes and providing there is a vacant skin. There are nineteen of these skins—Kiape, Soomia, Bugay, Tuna, Senyeri, Kasuape, Kunfosi, Buanfo, Bale, Daripe (Kulmasa), Seripe, Gelenoon, Konanipe, Jahori, Hanari, Karinson, Tarinyini, Grupe and Nakwaby. There is no promotion and no senior skin because seniority goes by age and relationship alone.

An Ewuriche is enrobed outside the Bolewura's compound and in front of all the Chiefs and Ewuriches who are present in the town and after the ceremony she is chaired to her compound in exactly the same way as a chief. When she is enrobed she sends presents to her village of salt for the women and kola for the men. In return they supply her with what foodstuffs they can afford, to provide the ceremonial "food for the dead" at the Damba Festival each year. An Ewuriche is under no obligation to live in her village or renounce her husband or children. Her post is now purely honourary. She has no jurisdiction over other women. In olden days, however, the Ewuriches used to have such jurisdiction and to sit with the Divisional Chief in cases involving women. They would also go to war with the army to cheer the soldiers on and to succour the wounded.

There are Ewuriches in other Divisions. In Kusawgu there is Zaw'wuriche and in Wasipe there is Buru'wuriche who has, however, no connection with the office of Buruwura. Buruwura has a female equivalent in Gbinipe'wuriche who was appointed through the richness, generosity and power of her brothers, but the appointment like that of Buruwura has now lapsed. The Ewuriches of other Divisions recognised her as their senior.

The Nyamase of the Bole Division are listed in Chapter 1. The owner of the land of Sakpa, Wakawaka, Maluwe, Tinga and Wasipe is Sakpawura.

Kademawura, a Vagella, is the Landowner of Bole. In olden days he, on behalf of the Nyamase, together with Mandarewura and Wulasiwura each gave a cow to Yabumwura at Damba. If he did not do so it was believed that evil and crop failure would result in Yabum. This present originally started as a gift between friends but with the years it hardened into a custom which was not altogether popular with the givers.

Kusawgu Division

The Kusawgu Division was the reward Ndewura Jakpa gave Wari, known as Kaluwi, his youngest and favourite son for conquering the Mpara tribes or, as the Dagombas know them, the Laisi. Indeed the very name of his Division "Fought" or "Obtained" commemorates Wari's achievement. The Mpara who are the Nyamase of this Division gradually adopted the Gonja language in preference to their own tongue which is now not even remembered. They still, however, own the land and tend the shrines of the local gods. They claim a wide kinship with the Tampluma and Mparaba peoples. The border of this Division marches with that of Dagomba and Kusawguwura numbers many Dagombas amongst his subjects, in fact, Dagomba is possibly the dominant language in the Division.

The constitution of Kusawgu deviates from the usual pattern in that the Royal Gonja line of Chiefs are eligible for two skins only, the Divisional skin itself and that of Yapei. There are four gate families to the

Kusawgu skin which take the name of the last man of that family to occupy the Kusawgu skin. The succession passes to each of these families in turn and is in the direct male line of each of them, for though the son of a Chief may became Kusawguwura, the brother of a Chief may not. In the old days a candidate succeeded to the skin direct from private citizenship. In 1939, Mam, the present Kusawguwura started the custom of giving the Yapei skin to the heir apparent. Yapei was a creation of the British and was originally a consolation prize for those of the Royal line who were not eligible for the Divisional skin. The appointment of a new Kusawguwura is made by Yabumwura and the successful candidate is enrobed by Kitowura who is the Nyamase Paramount Chief of the Mpara people and a very prominent elder. There is a Liman in Kusawgu, and Katcherasiwura is the Mbonwura.

As in Tuluwe the Divisional Chief does not need to live in Kusawgu. Soale, who later became Yabumwura, lived at Kushiedu, his own village and he was not the first to adopt this practice.

There are some interesting and important mounted drums in Kusawgu called Mbontikuribi, as there are at Tuluwe and Damongo.

Moslems

The association between the Gonjas and the Moslems is a long one which began when Ndewura Jakpa met Mallam Fatu-Morukpe before he set out on his conquests. Indeed Ndewura Jakpa's success is in part attributed to Fatu-Morukpe who with his wonder working staff held the fortune of battle in sway.

Fatu-Morukpe, whose name "Fatig-Morukpe" means "Moslem Elder," according to the Bole tradition was born in Mecca the son of Abu Bakari, son of Asumana of the Kamagte people of that city. He met the Ndewura at Mande and a friendship blossomed between the two. Ndewura Jakpa gave him a wife through whom the Mamagte or Sakparebi family (to which all the divisional Limans of Gonja belong) became related to the house of Jakpa. Rumour has it that Ndewura Jakpa gave Fatu-Morukpe a gift of a hundred of everything, but it is false. Ndewura Jakpa made promise of such a gift if Fatu-Morukpe helped him and he was successful in his wars, but despite his success Ndewura Jakpa never honoured his promise. He did, however, offer to divide his conquests equally between the Gonjas and the Moslems, but Fatu-Morukpe refused. He suggested instead that he would be content if the Kamagte or Sakparebi were privileged to pray for improvements and advise the Chiefs against doing wrong. Ndewura Jakpa agreed and ordered that in future the Chiefs must accept the advice tendered to them by their Limans. It is said that Fatu-Morukpe did not live long to follow his friend Ndewura Jakpa. He was succeeded by his son Mawule Fatigi who accompanied the Gonjas in their wars even to Nanumba.

Ndewura Jakpa, according to Buipe tradition, settled in Buipe which may indeed be true, because the Yabumwura's Liman used to be appointed from Buipe, but the custom lapsed after the disgrace of the last Liman of Yabum who could not read the Arabic script, and since then no other has been appointed. Ndewura Jakpa gave a Mallam to Kpembe, Buipe, Tuluwe, Janton, Kakpande and Kafaba.

Each of the divisions of Gonja has its own Liman who advises the Chief and keeps records in the Koran but if Bole is typical, these records cannot be very valuable as they only give the day and month of an event and not the year of the Hegira when it took place. The Moslems in the Divisions are very closely associated with Gonja customary observances and feasts though they keep the strictly Islamic feasts as well.

In *Yabum* there are two interesting Moslem villages of 'Mara' people. They are Larabanga and Dokrupe. Larabanga was founded by a Mallam called Braimah Laraba who visited Mecca and brought back with him the famous Larabanga Koran which is over two hundred years old. When he came to Gonja he was well received by Ndewura Jakpa who gave him gifts of slaves, chattels, and a place to settle at Larabanga. Later Nabori was colonised from Larabanga. Dokrupe was founded by Mallam Dokruja, a follower of Fatu-Morukpe from Reanu. The inhabitants of this group of villages are known as Kawogte amongst the Moslems.

The *Kpembe* Limans are of the Mamagte stock and succeed in order of seniority. There is only the one Kamagte family here. There were also the Mawule who traced descent from Fatu-Morukpe and the Sisi, who acquired their name which means "smoke" because on their way here Ndewura Jakpa and Fatu-Morukpe saw a column of smoke and met the Sisi who joined them in their adventures, but both these peoples are now extinct. There are some Jagbagtes in Kpembe.

Wasipe. Since Wasipewura's ill treatment of the Sakparebi long ago, the Daboya Liman has always been a stranger and not a Kamagte. This was Wasipewura's revenge. There are however, some Sakparebi living in Daboya.

Islam is strong in *Bole.* Its followers fall into two groups, those who came in with Mallam Fatu-Morukpe and those who were here before the Gonjas came. Of the Moslems who came in with Ndewura Jakpa and Fatu-Morukpe there are the Kamagte or Sakparebi and the Jagbagte who are the descendants of the wife who was given to Fatu-Morukpe by Ndesura Jakpa but are not his issue. The Limans of Bole succeed through either of the Kamagte families, the Karampe or the Dumangu, which are named after one Bole Liman and his brother who succeeded him. There is no further qualification for succession except faithful service and dead men's shoes. It may be of interest to note that the Kamagte and presumably the Jagbagte people came to Bole from Chama in Tuluwe. The present Bole Liman claims to be the tenth Liman since the move to Bole.

There are also the Dabos who have a central Gonja origin. They are the descendants of a man called Dabo who at the time of Ndewura Jakpa's invasion lived in a small village in the neighbourhood of Buipe. When Ndewura Jakpa came to this village he did not intend to stay there for he said "If I were to stay here my Moslems would have neither food nor water; God is great." Dabo, however, persuaded him to change his mind and when he had showed him a well of water, guinea corn for horse fodder and rice for the men to eat. Next morning when the army was about to move Dabo gave Ndewura Jakpa his eldest son to carry Fatu-Morukpe's blanket for him for the duration of the war. Dabo died before the war ended, but his son remained with Fatu-Morukpe as his father had wished. This first Dabo is said to have been a Moslem before his meeting with Ndewura Jakpa and Fatu-Morukpe.

Besides the Dabos in Bole there are others at Buipe and Kadelso and, descended through the female line, at Salaga. there are none in Daboya. Dabo has the duty of preceding the Liman whenever he visits a Chief's house and is his messenger to any Chief who contemplates wrong. He it is too who winds the turban of enrobement round a new Liman's head at the installation ceremony in front of the Chief's house. As a reward for all these duties Dabo is presented with the neck of the Bull given by the Divisional Chief to his Liman at Damba.The Moslems who were already in Bole when the Gonjas came were of the related Ligbi, Kurabari and Watera people. The Ligbis who are descended from Gondo and his younger brother Turugu came from Fugula through Bui and Dua (Banda Nkwanta) to Bole where they intermarried with the Gonjas. Many of the Dua Moslems are still Ligbi and there are also many Ligbis in Wenchi. The Kurabari came from Bouna and are descended from one Idrusu. The Watera who are descended from Alhaji Mama came from Segu where, having forcibly converted the Pagans to Islam, they made themselves Chiefs. All three tribes claim to have come to Gonja at the same time.

Besides Bole, there are Mosques and Limans in Mandare, Larabanga, Maluwe, Tuna and Dua all of which come under the Bole Liman, who in turn acknowledges the Buipe Liman as his senior. There is no promotion for Limans.

Law and Custom. In each of the Divisions the Liman, who is also an important elder of the Divisional Chief, settles disputes and resolves questions of law that are brought to him by his people.

Marriage follows orthodox Islamic practice, the essentials of which are the presence of witnesses and a contract specifying the bride price money—or goods—given by the groom or his father to the bride's father. A little girl may be promised to a man who will come to claim her when her parents think the time is ripe. Meanwhile he will keep them sweet by periodic small presents. Marriage is solemnised by the tying of the bridal knot or Furu by the Moslems of the town which is done to the accompaniment of readings from the Koran. Food is bought by the new husband and distributed to prominent people and he gives his wife a new cloth. A man may keep four wives at one time. In one respect, however, in Bole, and possibly elsewhere in Gonja, a radical departure is made from orthodoxy in that a Moslem woman is permitted to marry a Pagan husband. A marriage of this sort is permitted only between relatives and any issue of the match is illegitimate. This "illegitimacy" is really a quibble as in the view of the pagan father and his people the issue will be legitimate. In such a match after the birth of the third or fourth child the mother's father will come to ask for one of the children to train in the faith. If one is given him this child automatically becomes legitimate. Such a match would be a source of worry to strict Moslems.

Divorce procedure in Bole and probably elsewhere in Gonja differs in some respects from orthodox practice in which a man may obtain a divorce merely by repeating one of the recognised formulae thrice. A woman on the other hand may only divorce a man with his consent.

In Bole a man may obtain a divorce in either of two ways. (*i*) He can take his wife to the Liman and say—"I do not want you again. If I lie with you in the future it is as though I lie with my mother,"—which formula once said makes a divorce final, or (*ii*) He can take his wife to the Liman and explain before witnesses why he wants a divorce. If a woman's offence is adjudged bad he is asked if he wishes to keep her as his wife. He may then say to the woman three times—"I do not want you," after which the divorce is agreed upon, but he must pay her a small sum of money daily for three months to provide her food. This period is prescribed to ascertain if the woman is going to conceive a child. At the end of the period, the man, the woman and the witnesses are once more summoned before the Liman who asks—"What did you say three months ago?"

If the man repeats his desire for a divorce he makes an oath to that effect. Furu is then cut and a sum of money is paid to the woman. The cutting of Furu is an essential to legal divorce and that is why if a woman wants to divorce her husband she must first obtain his consent.

Any property owned by a woman at the time of her marriage or given to her by her husband during the marriage may be taken by her when the divorce is made absolute.

The History of the Kagbanya People

The task of trying to piece together a narrative history of an illiterate people is hard. In this instance there are four written sources which largely agree on main points, but these sources record the Moslem names of the Kings and Chiefs of Gonja whereas they are remembered in the District only by their Gonja nicknames. For after the accession of a Chief it is an offence to address him by his first name. The position becomes more confused because although the Divisional Limans often record the Chiefs' names in their Koran and read them over during the Damba Festival, it is the nicknames that are recorded while the Moslem name given to every Gonja by the Liman seven days after birth is forgotten. Hence the process of identifying the dramatis personae of the manuscripts with that of the oral tradition is difficult in the first place and made increasingly so as folk memory is apt to be inaccurate and local.

In constructing a history from such sources, the writer is obliged to clutch at straws and has to be contented with a finished work bearing more relationship to an illsewn patchwork quilt than an intricate tapestry of harmoniously blended colours. To avoid any charge of attempting to force facts, the four written sources whence I have drawn most of my material are included in the appendices to this essay, together with a list of persons who have given me verbal information. Thus the reader will himself be able to judge the validity of my deductions.

All manuscript and traditional sources agree that the Gonjas came from the Mande country to the North West of the Gold Coast. This is the story of their coming.

Gisi Jarra, the King of Mande Kabba, heard there was gold at Segou, so he sent messengers to the Chief of Segou to ask him to pay tribute in gold, but the Chief of Segou refused. The King of Mande Kabba therefore sent an army against Segou which razed the town and captured its Chief. Now in the army were two boys Maba'a and Imoru, sons of the King of Mande Kabba who made Imoru, the elder, Chief of Segou. When later a report reached Imoru that gold was to be found at Buna he sent for his brother, Naba'a, and told him the news and said "Gbonya Ka na," "Go and return quickly" which is the origin of the name Kagbanya or Gonja as it is now known.[1]

So Naba'a went and conquered Buna which he sacked, but instead of returning he pressed on Eastward across the Black Volta River at Ntereso to Wabili and Sakpa where the Chief arranged for the submission of the villages immediately West and South West of Bole. He continued his career of conquest until at length he was killed fighting the Nkoranzas.[2]

---

1 Another variation of the origin of the Gonja name is given on page 6 of "A Short History of Salaga" by J. Withers Gill. It is from the Hausa phrase *"Gun jan goro"* meaning "the land of red kola" as Buipe was once a centre of the red kola trade.

2 All dates in this chapter are according to the chronology of Mr. Jack Goody.

Now in the course of Naba'a's expedition a Moslem called Ismaila came to Buipe[3] with his son Mallam Mohamed Labayiru to salute him. The two were well received but Ismaila died at Sanfi on his way home. When the sad tidings were brought to Naba'a he sent money and gifts for the dead Moslem's obsequies. When these had been performed Mohamed Labayiru returned to see Naba'a his father's friend, but he found that in the meantime Naba'a had died and his son Manwura sat in his place. He met Manwura at Kawlaw one Friday while his forces were engaged in battle. The sun was very fierce so Mohammed Labayiru said "Let us go into the shade of that large tree," and Manwura replied "We cannot do so because it is too close to the fighting." Mohammed Labayiru rejoined "If God wills we will drive away the unbelievers and sit beneath the tree." Whereupon he arose and followed by Manwura walked to the tree, beat the ground with his leather headed staff and stuck it in the earth between the combatants. When the enemy saw this they fled and Kawlaw opened its gates to the Gonjas.[4]

So impressed was Manwura with the power of the Moslem's religion that he, his brothers and his nephews straightaway adopted Islam and received new names. Manwura was succeeded by Amoah Imoru Saidu Alhaj who ruled for twenty one years. He was followed by Jakpa Lanta who can be none other than Ndewura Jakpa, the great Gonja here and the subject of many legends.

Up to this time it seems that the Gonjas had not penetrated beyond the area round the confluence of the Black and White Voltas and had their base at Buipe. Now Ndewura Jakpa with his "band of brothers" by a series of decisive military campaigns established his way Northward towards Mamprussi and Eastward to beyond the Oti River. First he struck Northward to deal the death blow to Dagomba hegemony over the Tampluma in what is now the Wasipe Division by defeating the Dagomba army and slaying Na Dariziogo their King. Other sections of the Dagbon Empire were now ripe for plucking. After the defeat of Na

---

3 This is according to the Kanakulaiwura's MS., which I favour on the grounds that Buipe Liman is the senior of the kamagte or Sakpare Limans. The version of the Mande Kabba MS. is that Mohammed Labyiru met Naba'a at Segou. Another fact which makes me incline towards the Kanakulaiwura's MS. is that he mentions two Mallams—Ismaila and his son Mohammed Labayiru—and says that the first did not know Naba'a for long. This accords with oral tradition as related by Kpembe Liman in 1953 and seems further to point to the identification of Mallam Fatu-Morukpe, the founder of the Kamagte line, as Ismaila and his successor Mawuli Fatigi, who accompanied the Gonjas in their conquests even to Nanuma, as Mohammed Labayiru.

4 According to the Bole MS., Wam was the subjugator of Kawlaw and was later killed by the resurgent Nkoranzas. Lata according to the same source was also engaged against the Knoranzas and died at Kappasi, which seems to have been the Gonja base in these wars. Kapoasi is the gate to the Debre skin.

Dariziogo and possibly in the same campaign, the Gonjas pushed Eastward to receive the submission of the Mparaba Divisions of Panshiaw, Janton and Kakpande, and Ndewura Jakpa dispatched his youngest son to take the Mpara State of Kusawgu. Ndewura Jakpa returned once again to the confluence of the Voltas whence he probed into Kawlaw, received the submission of Kafaba, took Salaga and mounted a campaign against the Konkombas[5] east of the Daka River. This latter resulted in the capture of Alfai and even land beyond the Oti River in what is now French Togoland.

Besides being a great conqueror, Ndewura Jakpa was also a good organiser and administrator. He treated his new subjects kindly and appointed his relatives to rule them and to render a sort of feudal service as required. In this way with fairness and firmness he consolidated his conquests and founded the Gonja political system much as we know it today. Not content with his already extensive conquests, however, Ndewura Jakpa determined to make war upon Ashanti. His ambition killed him for it was during this war at Brumasi that he received the fatal wound from which he died at Siriminchu[6] as he was being carried homeward.

After Ndewura Jakpa it becomes exceedingly difficult to identify successive Yabumwuras, because in the Kanakulaiwura's manuscript, which is the only document that covers this post conquest period, only the Moslem names of Chiefs are given whereas oral tradition takes cognisance of their nicknames alone. Besides this, events such as famines and plagues which might give a vital clue, lie forgotten.

Ndewura Jakpa was succeeded by his son So'ara Sulimanu[7] who was Weurakung for the six years of Ndewura Jakpa's retirement to Buru[8] after which he reigned for sixteen years. He too was a warrior and made

---

5 There is a discrepancy here between Kpembewura Soali's history and the Bole MS. I have followed the former on the whole, because the general tradition states that the Nchumuru came in with the Gonjas in which case the Gonjas would not have found them there to fight. I mention the discrepancy because Manwura is named as the first Kpembewura in Kpembe Liman's Damba recital. Perhaps Manwura was indeed King during these wars when the Gonja Captains over-ran the land, but tradition insists that Ndewura Jakpa was the military genius who directed them.

6 There is said to be a guardian of the place where Nkewura Jakpa died at Siriminchu in his favourite son's arms. This is an interesting compromise account of the hero's death. The Buipe tradition and the Kanakulai MS. version that he died an old man in "Buru" gain support from "A Short History of Salaga" cited above, in which Ndewura Jakpa is said to have fought at Brumasi before the Kafaba incident and prior to his conquest of Kpembe and Alfai.

7 He may be the "*Sari*" father of Lanyon of Dasent's list. See Appendix II.

8 This contradicts the tradition of Ndewura Jakpa's death from a wound received while fighting the Ashantis and to that extent confirms the oral tradition of Buipe.

many conquests, but his people, who were tired of warfare and pined for peace, deposed him.

Now two short reigns intervene of Limu Imoru son of Ndewura Jakpa, brother of So'ara Sulimanu, and of Banga who had once been Sagiawura[9] in Wasipe, before a new light dawns upon the scene with the mention of Abbas[10] son of Ndewura Jakpa. Like his father he was a Moslem and a great leader who drew followers to his standard by his wisdom and the liberality which went hand in hand with his wealth. He outshone his brothers in all things.

Abbas waged war against the Chief of Longoro for twelve years before peace was made. Soon afterwards the Chief of Longoro died and for forty days Abbas shared power with Langa, his brother who then died leaving Abbas in absolute control. Abbas, however, did not occupy the Yabum skins until he had successfully waged war against Bouna when he was acclaimed, reigned one hundred days and died fighting against the Bandas at Fugula.

Mahama Labayiru of Kpembe succeeded Abbas and reigned for only two and a half years before he died. After this the Paramountcy declined in power and importance; each Divisional Chief set himself up as a petty King and if he felt so inclined waged war against his brothers. The brother of Abbas,[11] however, was the most powerful of these warring Chiefs and took precedence. He it was who killed the Ya Na and he died at Palari.

Now the times were very disturbed. Debrewura Sulugu was slain in a war between the Brong States of Techiman and Bondouku. In 1735–36, Kpembewura Sabalugu and his brother Murki Sumbungwura were defeated. Kandiawura Sangaragandi and the Kongwura, son of Osmanu, also died in Battle with the Dagombas when Mahamma Wari Kumpati was defeated and killed at Sanso. He was the Yabumwura's son and though not a Chief, was so great a favourite that no one dared announce the news of his death to his father who at length heard it from a wandering musician.

---

9 The Kanakulai MS. mentions "*Saywura*" in Wasipe, but no such title exists. There is, however, a "*Sagiawura*" in which word the "*g*" is hardly even sounded.

10 I put up the case that Abbas was Abase, first Tuluwewura, and Chief of a Division renowned for military prowess. Beside the similarity of names, it should be noted that the Kanakulaiwura's MS., from which the facts are taken, was written at Buipe and obtained by Kanakulaiwura "from a son of the Liman of Tuluwe," hence there was no need for its writer to record the fact that Abbas came from Tuluwe as he would presume his readers to have a knowledge of the affairs of Central Gonja; hence also his possibly excessive praise of Abbas' prowess. He also refers to Busunuwura the son of Abbas which fits in with tradition.

11 See Tamakloe's "A Brief History of the Dagbamba People."

In these middle decades of the eighteenth century, Gonja's Southern neighbours took advantage of internecine warfare to attack. Kpembe was harassed by the people of Kulasi,[12] and the people of Buipe fled before invaders from Daura.[13] Then the Ashantis invaded Gonja and Dagomba.

About this time a pestilence swept through the country and killed many people. It was followed by a plague of locusts and famine when the price of grain increased ten times and many people thought to leave the country. Next fell prodigious rains such as had been known only once before. Many houses were destroyed and the people made themselves grass shelters to live in.

Now Murki Kpembewura died and was succeeded by his nephew who eventually succeeded to Yabum.

The Weilas,[14] who were popularly known as Sunguipe, came to the large town of Bandaweila, the inhabitants of which fled, and the Weilas proceeded to the riverside where they settled. The locusts came again to Gonja this year.

Now the Weilas entered into a league with Kofi Suno and the Ashantis for the purpose of destroying and subjugating Gonja. Busunuwura, son of Abbas, heard of it and came to the river at Dikki to repel any attack. But all was quiet; Kofi Suno and his allies bided their time and when Busunuwura had gone they launched their attack. The Gonjas however defeated them and captured their leaders, while those who escaped fled to Dagomba which itself was rent by a civil war which enabled the Ashantis to occupy Yendi.

At about this time a dispute arose between Busunwura and Banda Yaw, who had killed one of Busunuwura's children, which somehow involved Yasowura son of the Chief of Wurape.[15] The dispute, had it been allowed to ripen, would have plunged the whole country into war, but Sulimanu, son of Abbas prevented it.

In Buipe, the brother of Buipewura Mahama Jarrawari seized the Silima skin from his younger brother, which deed shocked the local people because nothing of this nature had been done before.

At this time too Dagomba was in flames again and Savelugu Na sent to Wasipewura Sabunoyabung for succour against Karaga-Na Zibirim Kulunku, his rival for the Yendi skin. Wasipewura's army was defeated at Kumbungu and Osumanu, son of Kapoasiwura, son of Debrewura Sulugu died on the field. Save for their initial great successes under Ndewura Jakpa the Gonjas were not lucky in their wars with Dagbon.

---

12 Unidentified.

13 Unidentified.

14 These might be the Mo people who migrated from the vicinity of Tumu.

15 This is rather confused. *"Yasowura"* might be Yarizoriwura, in which event *"Wuripe"* would refer to Wasipewura. *"Wuripe,"* however, is a degree of Chiefship.

Now Jakpa, the Chief of Sansanne Mango, son of Sulimanu Chief of Kashiwu, and his brother the Chief of Longoro were defeated in Sansanne Mango with the people of that place who were their allies.

In 1764, Sulimanu Yabumwura, son of Abbas, died at Loha and was succeeded by his brother Abu Bakari,[16] son of Yabumwura Mustapha. Abu Bakari had been Kilibiwura from which he became Kpembewura and he was staying at Kulipe when the news of his promotion to Yabum came. His reign was only very short but during it he always remembered Kpembe with favour. Later that year he was succeeded by Yabumwura Osumanu's son, Abu Bakari, known as Lanyon amongst the Gonjas, who likewise had only a short reign.

There is now a gap in Gonja history until the end of the nineteenth century, when three events suddenly appear in the light of history. Firstly Babatu's slave raiding career had repercussions in Wasipe, next Kpembe was disturbed by the Kabache wars which established the Kanyasi family's rights of succession to the Division skin and finally the catastrophe of Samori's raid which immediately preceded the establishment of the British Protectorate smote Western Gonja.

Babatu himself had no dealings with the Gonjas though his career throws light on the affairs of Wasipe in the time of Wasipewura Takora in this way. When Babatu raided Walembele for slaves its people fled to Belele and Kundugu in Wasipe, repulsed their adversaries, and were thereafter allowed for seven years to practise their crafts in peace. They flourished, but Wasipewura Takora was angry because they had not paid him for his protection. He therefore seized two hundred and twenty of the refugees and sold them into slavery in lieu of payment. His brother Yarizoriwura Adama took up the refugees' cause and drove Takora from Daboya whence he fled to Dagomba. Takora remained in Dagomba for three years mustering forces to win back his Chiefship. This period might have been shortened had not the Zabaraimas whom Takora's son Zakariya had called to his father's aid been defeated and driven back to the North West.

Samori's raid is interwoven with the politics of Western Gonja and is linked with the name of Kongwuar Abudulai known as Kabondogodam. Kabondogodam was an ambitious and thoroughly unscrupulous man. He first usurped the Kong skins at the expense of Nantechi the rival claimant. Then on the death of Yabumwura Seidu in 1895 he determined to become the Paramount Chief himself. His claims may not have been received favourably or he may have been merely impatient, but he decided to call the slave raider Samori to his aid. Samori did not come himself but sent a well equipped army under his son. This army crossed the Black Volta River into Gonja at Ntereso South West of Bole where a

---

16 Half brother or brother in the wider sense of kinsman.

battle was fought. For some time the issue was in doubt, then the Gonja forces seized the advantage and pressed the invaders hard. Indeed had it not been that a section of Samori's army which was now brought into action, was armed with rifles it is likely that the invaders would have been repulsed. As it was the Gonjas gave way and fled to Jentilipe where they reformed and prepared to fight to the death. Meanwhile Samori's Captain divided his army. One section pursued the Gonjas to Jentilipe where it attacked the Gonjas who had taken their position in the village. The battle was fiercely fought. The attackers formed three concentric circles around the village. When the circle nearest the village had had enough it retired through the second which then took its place and similarly in its turn the second retired through the third. The first two waves were repulsed and ammunition was running short. Tradition says that the men of the third wave were obliged to load their guns with red peppers which they fired into the compounds. This was too much for the Gonjas whose leader Kabagali had been killed and they surrendered. Some managed to escape to the fastnesses of Knokori for the victors only pursued them as far as Kbolebi while others fled to Eastern Gonja.

Meanwhile the other section of Samori's army struck down to Benyalipe where it fought and defeated the Tuluwe army. After this battle Tuluwewura Jewu and many of his followers blew themselves up to avoid the disgrace of capture. Nevertheless the victors were able to send back a train of prisoners to Bole where the Headquarters had been set up. This section of the army remained in the region of Benyalipe to keep watch and ward Eastward and to report to Bole if war threatened from that direction. As things turned out this precaution was unnecessary because the news of Tuluwewura's defeat and death proved an effective deterrent to the re-enforcements that were on their way from Kpembe.[17]

After these battles the prisoners were brought to Bole where Kabon-dogodam pointed out the Gonjas and leading Nyamase who were led off to execution. Very many were put to death for this was a political war and not a slave raid, and there are two or three large mounds in the town beneath which the corpses were buried. Before leaving Bole for the North in pursuit of the fugitives, Samori's people laid waste the town which in those days was more populous than it is now. They did not penetrate to Wasipe which favoured the Kong cause or to Buipe, though they did advance to Busunu where they were defeated by the Gonjas and driven towards Wa, which may have been made possible because some of the Samori force had been withdrawn to meet the new threat of British arms. Samori's army met the Gonjas and others at Sankanna, it was driven to Mangu and thence to Samatigu where it encamped for three days. The mixed Gonja army attacked the Samori army by shooting arrows into the

---

17 The present Kpembewura who was a member of this expedition was my informant.

air which fell amongst the invaders who were hard pressed and only saved from defeat by the approach of night. When for some unaccountable reason[18] the mixed Gonja army retired during the night, Samori's captain decided to retire to Bouna. During his retreat many of his captive escaped.

The Samori Wars had caused great havoc and ruin in Western Gonja which now for the first time made the acquaintance of the British who began to pacify and reconstruct the country, but not before the Bole people had been able to wreck their revenge on Kong by razing it to the ground and massacring its inhabitants. Kabondogodam, however, had escaped to Bouna with Samori and some of his progeny, including Mama Moruwura, his eldest son, later settled in Kintampo while other Kongs sought refuge in Wasipe or on the Coast.

When the Protectorate was divided into convenient administrative units, however, Gonja suffered by the loss of the Kandia Division which stretched as far North as Walembele and was incorporated with other Gonja possessions in the Wala District. The Government was firm in its decision for in 1923 "the Chief of Tampluma who is either Kandi's eldest son or brother" was not allowed to attend the General Gonja Conference held at Yapei and because of his determination to attend was detained in the guard room at Wa.

---

18 The present Bole Liman was my informant. He was a captive of Samori's army at the time and witnessed these events.

APPENDIX I. PERSONS ENROBING
DIVISIONAL CHIEFS

Yabum	Kagbapewura
Kpembe	Kpembe Liman
Kusawgu	Kitowura
Wasipe	Jangbologuwura
Tuluwe	Chefijiwura
Bole	Kajumowura
Buipe	

APPENDIX II. THE REIGNS OF THE CHIEFS OF GONJA,
AS GIVEN IN THE KANAKULAIWURA'S MANUSCRIPT*

Naba'a	1566/7**	–	1595/6**	
Nawura Sa'ara	1595/6**	–	1614/5**	
Amoah	1614/5**	–	1634/5	
Jakpa Lanta	1634/5	–	1675/6	Became Chief of Bura d. 1681/2
So'ara	1675/6	–	1697/8	Deposed
Limu	1697/8	–	1697/8	Died
Banga	1697/8	–	1698/9	Died

Interregnum

Abbas	(100 days)		1709	Killed
Mahama Labayiru	1709	–	1713/4	Died
Sulimanu		–	1764	Died
Abu Bakari I	1764	–	1764	Died
Abu Bakari II	1764	–	1765	

* I am indebted to Mr. Jack Goody from whose manuscript work on the "Ethnology of the Northern Territories of the Gold Coast" I obtained the above list.

** These dates might be two years early.

YABUMWURAS ACCORDING TO THE BOLE DISTRICT
RECORD BOOKS: DASENT'S LIST

Lanyon eldest son of Sari
Mama son of Lanyon, reigned 55 years
Sabalagu   from Kpembe resigned
Jan   "   Tuluwe
Jakpa   "   Kusawgu
Nantechi   "   Kong
Seidu   "   Bole
Abudu   "   Bole died March 1908
Issaka   "   Bole died December 1908
Mama   "   Bole resigned
Lanyon   "   Seripe deposed 1902
Mama   "   Bole re-elected

Yapei Meeting of 31/3/1930 – 2/4/1930

Buru Lanyon from Senyon
Jewu   "   Tuluwe
Mama   "   Kusawgu
Wari   "   Kong 1870?
Adama   "   Kong
Mama   "   Kpembe
Seidu   "   Bole 1895
Abudu   "   Bole died 1908
Darimanu   "   Tuluwe appointed Lanyon Seripewura
                    as Regent. His own promotion was not
                    notified to the Administration as Tuluwe
                    is in the Salaga District.
Mama   "   Bole falsely elected
Mama   "   Bole later properly installed

Since 1930

Iddi Banbanga "   Tuluwe
Soale Lanyon   "   Kusawgu
Ewuntoma   "   Wasipe. The present Yabumwura (1954)

APPENDIX III. BUIPEWURAS ACCORDING TO KANAKULAI-
WURA'S MANUSCRIPT

Osumanu	1711/12
Mahama Soara	1718/19
Osumanu	1724/25 died, his brother succeeded
Mustapha	1724/25 – 1727/28 his brother succeeded
Latape	1727/28 – 1734/35
Abu Bakr	d. 1735/36
Mahama	d. 1737/38 nicknamed Babalura and brother of Latape
Saidu Lantabi	1737/38 – 1742
Mahama Jarrawari	1750/51

BUIPEWURAS ACCORDING TO MALLAM ALIFU OF BUIPE
TAKEN DOWN BY MR. E.A. MAHAMA IN 1953

1. Yafa
2. Konkonfri
3. Lebu
4. Dinkeri
5. Safu
6. Adama
7. Jinapo
8. Mushe
9. Saaka
10. Mahama the present Buipewura (1954)

Appendix IV. List of Kpembewuras
from Kpembe Liman's Manuscript

1. Manwura
2. Ewurakakur
3. Jakpa
4. Sabalagu
5. Bori—probably Yaya raised to Yabum and later to Buru, hence this name (Soali's MS.)
6. Timu
7. Jakpa
8. Jeje
9. Isanurafu
10. Bambanga
11. Lanyon
12. Napo
13. Dosi
14. Wayo
15. Jakpa
16. Jawulla—Abudulai Jawulla? 1728/29
17. Kali—Sumbung gate
18. Napo
19. Jakpa
20. Sabalagu—Lepo gate.
    Possibly Hussein Sabalugu? d. 1727/8.
21. Dosi—Sumbung gate
22. Sabalagu—Lepo gate. See Appendix IX
23. Bambanga—Sumbung gate
24. Napo—Lepo gate
25. Issifu Isanurafu—Kanyasi gate
26. Ninchubore
27. Timu
28. Kali
29. Jawulla—Lepo gate
30. Isanurafu—Kanyasi gate. The present Kpembewura (1954)

APPENDIX V. WASIPEWURAS ACCORDING TO
KANAKULAIWURA'S MANUSCRIPT

Al Hadj	died 1723/4
Abudulai	died 1730/1
Abu Bakr	died 1745/6
Mohamedu	1745/6

WASIPEWURAS ACCORDING TO DABOYA LIMAN, 1932

This was checked by me and continued from 23 to 28 in 1954.

1. Denya
2. Asura
3. Jakpa
4. Kumburi
5. Sabuyaro—probably Sabunoyabung who met his death at the battle of Kumbungu. See Tamakloe's "A Brief History of the Dagbamba People" p. 38.
6. Asafo Abudu
7. Tiperi Sawli
8. Gariba
9. Tulimi Kasa
10. Denyan II
11. Kankaranfo Soali
12. Nazim
13. Chanchanko Abudu
14. Saparapa Abudu
15. Takora Saidu (circa 1895, See Tamakloe's "A Brief History of the Dagbamba People," p. 53)
16. Abu Daramani Korfi
17. Darafu
18. Adama Asi
19. Saparapa Sawli
20. Tuluwi Kasa Adama
21. Wasipe Wuripe Mahama
22. Saparapa Mimuni
23. Chanchanko Mbeima (1928)
24. Tiperi Bakari
25. Mahama—the bad who was sent to prison
26. Ewuntoma—elevated to Yabum
27. Bakari Denyanwiri
28. Mama Sarfo—the present Wasipewura (1954)

APPENDIX VI. TULUWEWURAS ACCORDING TO SALAGA DISTRICT BOOK

Abase	4th son of Jakpa
Joru	Kalipe
Kakure	Kalipe
Jewu	Jewupe
Danga	Kalipe
Bambaya I	Kalipe
Kwaja	Jewupe
Sulemana	Jewupe
Yahu	Kalipe
Jaga	Jewupe
Bambaya II	Kalipe
Braimiah	Jewupe
Alhassan	Kalipe
Dawudu	Jewupe
Abudu	Kalipe
Jakpa I	Jewupe
Bwansa	Jewupe
Derimani	Kalipe d. 11/9/14
Jakpa II	Jewupe –/10/14 – 23/3/15
Seidu	Jewupe 1/5/15 – 16/10/24
Issaka	Kalipe 7/12/24 – 14/12/24
Iddi	Kalipe 18/5/25 – 1937 elevated to Yabum
Mama Bambaya	Jewupe 1937 – 1940 deposed
Adama	Kalipe 1940 – 1948
Diiwura	Jewupe 1948 the present Tuluwewura (1954)

APPENDIX VII. BOLEWURAS ACCORDING
TO BOLE DISTRICT RECORD BOOKS

1. Buru Lanyon promoted 1st Yabumwura
2. Wayo
3. Jakpaseie reigned 11 years
4. Denkaili reigned 7 years
5. Amantana reigned 9 years
6. Adama reigned 16 years
7. Seidu promoted Yabumwura
8. Amankwa reigned 8 years
9. Mumuni reigned 7 years
10. Denbwangu killed at Jentilipe
11. Kotobiri circa 1895
12. Abudu promoted Yabumwura
13. Iasaka promoted Yabumwura died on
     way to Nyanga 1908.
14. Mama promoted Yabumwura 1912
15. Yaya deposed and exiled 1918
16. Nantoma died 1928
17. Takoro

A LIST OF BOLEWURAS COLLECTED BY SOALI
MAMA BOLE INTERPRETER IN 1953

1. Kwajah
2. Saafu
3. Mama
4. Abudu Sei
5. Amantana
6. Adama Jarga
7. Kankan-Ninji
8. Mumuni Korgor
9. Digbangor
10. Kotobiri
11. Abutu Pontonporong promoted to
    Yabumwura
12. Saaka Diaboah—1908
13. Yaya Jarmani—1912
14. Mama Dangbonga who became Yabumwura
    Mama 1910
15. Jobadi Natorma 1918–28
16. Takora Adama 1928–36
17. Mama Awusi 1936 the present Bolewura
    (1954)

APPENDIX VIII. KUSAWGUWURAS ACCORDING
TO NYAGRI KUSAWGUWURA, TAKEN DOWN BY
MR. E.A. MAHAMA

Dinkeri Wari—Wari Kaluwi ("Wari the
    Youngest")
Bure Iddrisa
Salemana—later Yabumwura
Mumuni Manwule
Amafu
Dinkeri II
Soale Awurbi
Adama
Mumuni II
Gbiadese
Wurpe
Soale II
Nyagri—the present Kusawguwura (1954)

Appendix IX
The Kanakulaiwura's Manuscript

In the name of God the Compassionate, the Merciful, in remembrance of the people of old, and the Father of the Malam Mahama Labayiru, son of Ismaila who came with his son to the town of Ghofe[1] and how he came to the King of Gonja whose name was Naba'a, he came to the King of Gonja who was at war in Kafiashi[2].

He was received with honour and when they were going back to their town he Ismaila died, God have mercy on his soul, before they reached the town, he died at Sanfi and the news of his death was brought to his friend Naba'a.

They said "your friend the Malam Ismaila, verily he is dead," and so the King sent much money to his brother at Ghofe to offer prayers and to give alms.

They offered prayers and the people of the country of the blacks saw this and did likewise, each one making prayer and giving alms as he was able.

Then they took his son, who was also a Malam, Mohamed Labayiru,[3] and he went to the King, the friend of his father in friendship. He did not find him alive, he found his son Mawura who sat in the place of the King Naba'a.

He found him at Kolo,[4] and that day a Friday he found him fighting fiercely.

The midday sun was also strong and they were fighting in the sun, but he (the Malam) saw a large shady tree close to the scene of battle.

So the Malam (Mohamed Labayiru) said to the King of the Gonjas, let us go under the shade of the tree.

---

1 This is the old form of Buipe.

2 The "Country of the Blacks."

3 "The White One" Arabic.

4 This may be Kawlaw.

The King of Gonja replied "How can we get the opportunity to go and sit under the tree, it is close to the fight, so we cannot do so."

The Malam replied Insha Allahu (if God wills) we will drive off the unbelievers and we will sit at the foot of the tree.

Then the Malam went in front and the Ing of the Gonjas followed until they came underneath the tree.

The Malam carried a staff in his hand, its head was covered with leather.

He planted it in the ground, he struck the ground and planted the staff in the earth between the combatants.

Thus he did, and when the enemy saw this, they fled; by the power of God did he this.

When they (the Gonjas) opened the gates of Kolo, they entered the town and when the King of Gonjas saw what the Malam had done, he was astonished and he said "Behold the religion of these people surpasses our own."

Thus the Gonjas were envious and wished to enter into Islam.

So the King became a Moslem, together with his brother by name Amoah, with Limu, and with Jafa and Mafa, the twins, who were the sons of a Moslem.

His brothers Amoah and Limu died, at that time Mafa and Jafa were children and they were the nephews of the King (Mawura).

When they grew up they followed in the faith of their uncle Mawura the King of Gonjas.

When they repented the Malam gave them new names.

Now the Mawura's name was Sa'ara, and the Malam gave him the name of Imoru Kura. The name of Amoah was also Imoru, and Limu was called Imoru Saidu (Imoru the happy) and Jafa was called Al Hassan but Mafa was called Al Hussein.

They all repented on the same day.

Naba'a ruled for thirty years before he died, and his successor ruled for nineteen years.

He built the Mosque at Ghofe (Buipe) and Amoah was called also Al Haj, because he gave money to one to go and represent him in pilgrimage.

He went and prayed there and returned (to Ghofe) and so Amoah became Alhaj, and he (Amoah Imoru Saidu Alhaj) became King and ruled for twenty-one years.

But the Malams dispute this and say he ruled for two years more.

Now behold Lanta, who was Jakpa, entered into Bura.

When he was king he became very powerful, of all those who had gone before him, not one could equal him as a ruler, and everything concerning his kingdom he took into his hands, and he divided the country of Gonja, and gave to his brothers.

When he became king there was no one who dared dispute with him, and the power has remained in the hands of his brothers even to the present day.

When he died in the year of Hegira 1093,[5] so the Malams say, he had ruled for forty-two years.

He was very old and when he was ready to take the chieftainship of Bura, he handed over his kingdom to his son, who was called So'ara after his grandfather, but he was also called So'ara Sulimanu.

He was the son of Lanta, and he had ruled only for six years when his father died in Bura. After this he ruled for sixteen years. His rule lasted twenty-two years, until he was deposed.

While he reigned he conquered many lands and made war on many towns, and because there was continual war he was deposed.

The Malams say that when he was deposed it was in the year of the Hegira 1100.

His son was dead and his brother Limu succeeded him.

He took the name of Imoru son of Lanta and ruled for two months and fifteen days until he was killed.

After him came his brother called Banga, who had been chief of Saywura (close to Daboya) and after eight months he died.

If you do not know Saywura, it is the place near Wasipe (Daboya).

In this year a Malam Osman son of Alihu was killed and he was well known and liked by the people.

His brother who was left remained at the Mosque of Buipe to look after it.

At the end of this year the Liman Alhaji died, God have mercy on his soul, he was the son of a real Malam, the son of Mahama Labayiru.

Then came war between Abbas and the Chief of Longo,[6] in which many people were killed when brother killed brother, and those who were left had no strength remaining in them. Their villages disappeared likewise their power, and this lasted for twelve years, until peace was made between them.

Then the Chief of Longoro died, and the power remained in the hands of Abbas and his brother Langu.

Forty days after this Langu died and the power was left in the hands of Abbas at Garansu.

But Abbas would not sit in the seat of Government until the time came for him to die, although he kept the power always in his hands.

---

5 After many of these dates the translator has given his conversion to the Christian Chronology. I have omitted these as I stand by Mr. Jack Goody's dates, *vide* Appendix II.

6 Probably Longoro.

He sat in the seat of the Chief for a hundred days and then Tinaur[7] came and killed him.

Abbas said, "I will be a ruler" and he made for himself a powerful kingdom, no one withstood him.

Behold his power which was as the might of his father, his father a strong man of the sons of Lantar.

And in the time of Abbas many people came to follow him, exceeding those in number who had followed those who had gone before him. In power and in lands, exceeded he all his brethren, their riches and their expenditure also did he surpass.

He surpassed his brethren in intelligence, in beauty and in religion, as a believer he did even as his father Lanter who was Jakpa.

Therefore his power during his reign exceeded everything, even unto the present day, and unto this day his children still hold the power.

Behold Abbas the victorious, even he made war on, he conquered Guna (Buna).

Guna is a large city, half way from Guna to the Conja country is the town called Ghofe, it is a ten days journey and there is a river in between.[8]

On the day that he destroyed Buna, on that day was Abbas hailed as King of the Gonja.

He had a Malam called Sherif, and on that day Abbas gave him gold to the weight of twelve miskals, in the name of God he gave him alms.

And he gathered together all the Malams who were following Sherif and gave them alms, a hundred miskals.

He (Abbas) gave thanks to God because of the booty he had obtained from Guna (Buna). How much gold was there he did not know, it was known only to God.

After Guna, he made war against Fula,[9] a town in the rocks (hills) in the country of Gonja, from Fula to Ghofe is four days for a quick walker and five for a slow one and a river lies between.

The King went with his brothers to Fula where thanks to the help of the Moslems they were victorious, but in the victory Abbas was slain.

This was in the month of Rabillawa the fifteenth day of the month in the year of the Hegira 1121.

Twenty-two years after this his brother Mahomadu, Chief of Kom[10] died, twenty-three years after the Chief of Diki died, and his little father

---

7 The Tonawa or Ashantis.

8 The Black Volta.

9 Probably Gugula, a town of the Bandas.

10 Probably Kong.

(uncle) succeeded and he was called Mahama Labayiru of Kombi,[11] son of Lantar.

He succeeded to Yabum.

After the death of Abbas no one ruled for any length of time.

Mahama Labayiru, may God have mercy on him, ruled only two and a half years when he died. After his death, the kingdom was no longer in the hands of one, but all had their own, towns and the country was divided.

Now the most powerful was the brother of Abbas, he took precedence over all, and was the king of kings.

The affairs of the kingdom were in the hands and are so until the present day.

Twenty-three years had passed after Abbas when Osmanu became Chief of Ghofe.

Twenty-five years after a town called Tounouma[12] was destroyed by war and twenty-six years after (the death of Abbas) the Chief of Yendi was slain.

In the twenty-ninth year (after the death of Abbas) the brother of Abbas killed the chief of Yendi and he died at Kpalari.

In the thirty-first year died Mahama So'ara, son of Lantar, and he was Chief of Ghofe.

In the thirty-third year died the Malam Mahama Konadi, and the Chief of Tuluwe Mahama, son of Abbas.

In the thirty-fifth year came war from Bawo to Tekiman, they came, they shot at the men of Tekiman and killed them.

In this was the Chief of Debre was slain, his name was Sulugu.

In the thirty-sixth year died Al Hajji Chief of Wasipe.

In the thirty-seventh year died Osmanu Chief of Ghofe and his brother Mustapha succeeded him.

In this year went Sulimanu and Abu Bakr, sons of the Chief (Gonja) to Mecca, and one Malam Mahama Bunayi died at Suna.

At the close of the thirty-ninth year died Malam Basa Karamoko, his proper name was Al Hussein, son of Al Hajji Laminu.

In the forty-first year died Abudullahi Jowalla and in the forty-third year died Malam Mawuli Pettigi Mahama, Mahama Saidu son of Sa'adu, son of Mustapha, son of Mahama Labayiru, and Abudullahi Chief of Wasipe died.

In the forty-fourth year diekd Imoru, son of Al Hajji Laminu, who was called also Basa Karamoko.

In that year our father Mustapha went to Mecca, in the month of Ragal, he went to Mecca on a Thursday the twenty-seventh day of the month.

---

11 Kpembe.
12 Bimbilla.

Now in this time the people of Mango were called Zuma.

In the forty-fifth year died our father Mustapha on whom be peace, he died on the twenty-first day of the month of Moharram. He died at Yadinati close to the town of Katsina.

Oh! Hear the words of the Malam, father of Al Hajji Mohamed Labayiru.

In his talk he tells us how the Gonja had their origin.

In this year came the men of Bawo and fought with the people of Gonja.

In the fortieth year Al Hajji Mahama return from Mecca and in this year Mustapha Chief of Ghofe died and his brother Latape sat in his place.

After that died Hussien Chief of Kombi whose nickname was Sabalagu.

In the forty-seventh year died Latape Chief of Ghofe.

He had a brother whose nickname was Babalura.

In the forty-eighth year died Abu Bakr Chief of Ghofe.

In the forty-ninth year Sulimanu returned from Mecca, and Al Hajji Mahama.

In this year the people of Kombi were destroyed by war and the Chief called Karbuwura, and his brother Sabalugu was with him and his brother Murki, Chief of Sunbung. In this year died the Liman Mustapha known as Bajaberidi, and Abdul Arramanu an ancient Arab and Imoru Saidu, who had been a commander of the soldiers of Abbas; he was Chief of the horses.

Sangaragandi chief of Kandia died, he was killed in the war, also the Chief of Kom, son of Osman, who was afterwards Chief of Chofe.

He was killed in battle together with our grandfather Malam Fadabiga.

In the year of the Hegira 1150 died Mahama Chief of Ghofe, who was called Bobalara.

After came Saidu, son of Laga, known as Lantabi.

In the fifty-first year died Abu Bukr called Yegi. He was the son of Malam Imoru Konandi.

In the fifty-third year died Salifu, son of a Chief, and brother of Al Hajj Sulimanu.

In the fifty-fourth year in the month of Zulhadj died Saidu called Latabi also Atabin, master of the Hobbling ropes, and it said he had been so for fifty-nine years.

In the fifty-fifth year died Imoru Konandi, son of Al Hajj Lamina, who was known as Bara Karamoko.

During his time Sulimanu son of Abbas was king.

During the month of Rabilawa in the fifty-sixth year the people of Kombi fled on account of the pagans of Kulasi, an din the fifty-seventh year the people of Ghofe fled before the pagans of Daura.

At the end of this year the infidels entered into the country of Gonja and the Gonja knew them as Imbo.[13]

They also invaded Gwong[14] and the people of Gwong took to flight, in the month of Zulhadj the month of prayer.

In the fifty-eighth year died Mohomadu while he was coming to his brother Mohammed Basa Karamoko.

Mohama Konandi became Liman of Ghofe and Asheka died an old man on whom be peace.

On the twenty-second day of the month of Rabilawa a Thursday, Salifu son of Lamina returned from Mecca.

Abu Bukr, Chief of Wasipe died and was succeeded by the son of his younger brother, Mohomadu son of Al Hajj. Then came a sickness which killed many people in the country of Gonja and there came also a famine and there was no food. The people were about to fly from the country and a measure of corn was sold for one hundred and fifty cowries.[15]

The weight of the prophet was five hundred.

In this year the locusts came in great numbers and all the people feared lest their crops should be destroyed.

But nothing was destroyed in their town,[16] and the locusts passed over.

In this same year the rain fell exceedingly heavily, and many houses were destroyed, behold the water its volume was as it was once of old, but the houses did not fall.

However the people feared that they would lose their houses and they made shelters of grass.

In this year Murki, King of Kombi died and his nephew succeeded him, and he came and succeeded to Yagbum.

In the fifty-ninth year died Al Hajj Sulimanu son of Lamina.

On the 30th night of Zulhadj when the moon was thirteen days, the Chief of Buna was captured, called Malba, son of Ali Mora, son of Alhadj Lamina, known as Basakaramoko. He was captured and he was roughly treated before he was killed.

In the sixtieth year the Liman died, Harrawari, son of Saidu Imoru, son of Mustapha, he died on the eighteenth day of the month of Mohorram.

---

13 Ashantis.
14 Dagomba.
15 Fifteen cowries would be the normal price.
16 Buipe.

The Liman was called Imoru Bunasoma.

Imoru son of Osman son of Soma, son of Kurfa, son of Mahama Labayiru became Liman.

In this year the infidels called Weila came, the people of Gonja knew them as Sunguipe.

The pagans came into the big town of Bandaweila and the men of Bandeweila ran away. They came to the bank of a river where they met with a man called Dandebo, he had a brother called dalibada, they saw him in his farm harvesting his corn.

They shot him with guns and hit him in the thigh, they shot him also in his testicles and he fell on the ground but his bones were not broken.

They beat him on the head with axes and on his throat, and he slept a little before he died.

It was on the twelfth day of the month Lahiya that the locusts came and ate the corn of many people.

In the sixty-first year Soma died and the Chief of Busunu, son of Abbas came to Dikki on the river, he came on account of the people of Weila.

They came with Kofi Suno, because they (the Gonjas) had killed his father's brother. They the people of Baso[17] had killed his father's brother amongst the farms of Gwo (Dagomba).

The people of Weila wished to destroy Gonja.

The people across the river (Volta) wished to take the country of Gonja and put it under their own rule, and because of this the Chief of Busunu embarked on the river and went against them.

But they made no further move and remained quite, nor did they do any evil against the country of Gonja.

And the Chief of Busunu sat down at Dikki, he remained there a month, but the people feared and did no more wrong.

So he returned with his brother Sulinanu Salinga, a rich man.

In this year they (Weilas) killed a man of Mango, Alhadji Yakubu, son of Jima of Mango, the mercy of God on his soul.

His brother Abu Bukr saved himself in time, he did not even wait to bury his brother.

In a little while Kofi Suno came again with the people of Weila, the Gonjas killed many of them including the slayers of Alhadji Yakubu.

They captured their leaders and troubled them greatly.

Those who remained fled to Dagonguraga (Dagomba).

In the sixty-second year war broke out again between the Dagombas of Dagonguraga and the rest of Dagomba.

They slew each other in great numbers, but the people of Dagonguraga were stronger than the others.

---

17 Gonjas.

Their farms were in between them and Gurugna was victorious and waxed powerful.

The people of Gwo returned with Kofi Suno and drove away the Dagonguraga from their town together with the people of Mango.

They said "El Mahdulillahi" we have driven away the people of Gurugu.

And in this month the Dagonguraga Na ran away.

In this was died Abu Bukr, son of the Chief of Busuna, son of Al Hadji Lamina Sankaramon.

On a Friday night the thirteenth of the month of Jimada Lahiru in the sixty-third year there was an eclipse of the moon and on a Thursday the twenty-first day of the month of Mohorram there befell an eclipse of the sun.

In this month on the same day died Ayi, son of Ayi King of Ashanti (Mulki Asanti) may God curse him, may he cast his soul and cast it into the fire.

He it was who troubled the people of Gonja, continually and at all times did he trouble them, he seized their possessions, whatever he wished so he did for he was all powerful in his rule, in his pride and conceit he loved to interfere with the business of others.

And all his people feared him and feared him greatly.

The power of his rule endured for a long time, and after forty years he died and his uncle's son whose name was Kayishi, he succeeded Ayi.

A dispute arose between the Chief of Busunu, son of Abbas and one Banda Yaw and a Chief called the Yasowura, Abu Bukari, son of the Chief of Wurape.

The deed done by Banda Yaw was proclaimed in every town for he had killed a child of the Chief of Busunu.

Everyone made ready for war and the people were all much afraid for they no longer wanted war in Gonja as in former days in the creating of Gonja; "God save us from war as in the olden days gone by."

They knew that if they fought as in the olden times, if (the war) would never finish, as it was the kind of fighting that would involve the whole land.

So Sulimanu, son of Abbas prevented war, he and his brother they were the Chiefs.

These affairs were not good if they brought war to the land of Gonjas.

Behold how the people fought of old, we pray God not to send wars again among the Moslems. God help our country, God helped them because of Mahama, Chief of Wurape.

He came to the Chief of Busunu, he settled it (the palaver), there was no more evil.

About this time the month of fasting died Hussein brother of Yunusa and in this year the people of Dagonguragu fled to the Chief of Gwona (Buna).

Together with Kofi Suno, the men of Gwo passed them to Gwona.

Then the Chief of Dagonguragu begged the Chief of Gwona to settle the matter between himself and the people of Gwo, but this he could not do and the fighting between them started once more.

The Chief of Gwona was slain by them, may God curse him, may God cast his soul into the flames together with his brethren, may God cast their souls into the fire (Nari) and those of all their people.

The brother of Dagonguraguna may his soul also be cast in the flames.

He met his end in the war, he was as the father of the Dagonguraguna.

Then the people returned to their town and all these happenings took place in the month of fasting.

In this same month was killed a man from Mango called Fogamajima, the brother of Shehu.

In the sixty-fourth year Salifu died, God give him peace, and he was the Chief of Kapuyare.[18]

Mahama Jarrawari was the Chief of Buipe.

On the thirtieth morning of the twenty-third day of the moon in the month of Safa, his brother sat on the skin of Sarrama,[19] he took it from the hand of his younger brother.

He was called Al Hadji, and on that day the people were greatly astonished, saying "We have never seen such tings."

In that month a Chief of Kombi died, who was called Murki, son of Kombi Sabalugu, and formerly he had been the Kanakulaiwura.

His little father succeeded to a town called Nakamawula.

He was also the son of Kombi Sabalugu.

He Murki, son of Lantar, Chief of Kombi whom they called Jakpa.

After him came one Osumanu, son of the Chief of Kupugari19 son of the Chief of Debre, called Salawu.[20]

He died in battle in the month of Jimadu Lahiru, near Kombungu close to the Gurma country.

They were together with Jakpa (in the war) and Jakpa was the Chief of Sansanne. He Jakpa, the son of Sulimanu, Chief of Kashiwu,[21] his

---

18 Possbily Kapoasi in Debre.

19 Silima: a gate skin to Buipe.

20 Probably Sulugu above.

21 Possibly Kusawgu. See Appendix VIII.

brother was the Chief of Longoro, and they were all gathered together in Mango.

In that month they were destroyed by war, they and the people of Mango were utterly destroyed by war.

During this year in the middle of the month of Sha-aban the Chief of Fula died, his name was Shitayi and he had ruled for thirty-one years.

This was in the year of Hegira 1176.

In the ninth month of the following year died Sulimanu, son of Abbas, King of Gonja, may God have mercy on his soul.

On a Tuesday at Loha he died. His brother Abu Bukari, son of Mustapha King of Gonja succeeded him; it was on a Friday the twenty-seventh day of the month of Layia Zulhadji.

Now this all happened before the things that I have written, and at the time Abu Bukari, son of Mustapha, King of Gonja, had a very powerful kingdom.

The twenty-ninth day of Ramadan, the month of the fast called Marisu was a Thursday, and on a Friday came the 1177th year of the Hegira.

On a Sunday on the thirteenth day of the month of Rabillahu died Abu Bukari, son of Mustapha, King of Gonja.

He died at sunset when the sun was no longer hot.

Abu Bukari, he made indeed a powerful kingdom of the country of Gonja, formerly he was Chief of Kombi and before that he sat at Kulipe.

In the year of the Hegira 1178 he was at Kulipe and after eight months he was called on to take the Chiefdom of Yagbum. What is written here is indeed the truth.

And because he had sat once at Kombi, there was always much friendship between Abu Bukari son of Mustapha and the people of Kombi, how much no one could know save God.

After him came Abu Bukari son of Osumanu as King of Gonja.

In the year of the Hegira 1178 on a Friday twenty-third day in the month of Jimada Loune he began to rule and ended on a Friday on the twenty-seventh day of the month of Fast called Akutobar in the year of the Hegira 1179.

These are the words of the two old men, two Malams, of whom one was called Liman Imoru Konandi, son of Imoru, and the other Alhadji Mohama, son of Mustapha, and the things which God caused to happen, how the Gonjas had their origin in the reign of Naba'a with the doings of the Moslems Ismaila and his son Mahama Labayiru and of the King of Gonja and all the Kings of Gonja up to the time of the rule of Abu Bukari, son of Osmanu whose nickname was Layu, but the Gonjas all called him Layon.

The writings of Mahama, son of Abudallahi.

The words of our forefathers, God have mercy upon them and their descendants the Moslems.

Appendix X
The Mande Kabba Manuscript

A Mallam that I have been trying to get hold of for more than two years has recently returned to Bole from his travels and this evening he came to see me in Bole with an old Arabic manuscript.

It contains an account of the coming of the Gonja dynasty and a link necessary in my history, so we spent a very profitable and pleasant evening.

This extract from my diary is dated 2 October 1932. The second version I obtained from another document.

Sgd. A.C. Duncan-Johnstone.

Version No. 1

In the name of the Compassionate, the Merciful.

This is about the forefathers of Gbanya and the things which came to pass in their country and the war fought by their Chief, Fiji, nicknamed Jarra. He was Chief of Mande-Kabba[1] and his was a great kingdom in the country of Mande. He heard the news of gold in the country of Segu[2] where it grew out of the ground like grass, by the grace of God. The gold was kept in two houses, which had no doors. Because of this, two messengers were sent to the Chief of Segu. They told him that the Chief of Mande sent a message about the gold: "This gold you pick up and sell every year," they said, "You did not send any to the Chief of Mande, your father. Why don't you give any to him?. Because of your own greatness you should give some to him. If you do not, he will take it by force."

---

1 Kangaba. Capital of the Mande (Mali) Empire.
2 Part of the Mande Empire.

The Chief of Segu looked at the two messengers, and said, "I will never give him any."

The Chief of Segu sent the two messengers to the Chief of Mande to tell him these words.

They recounted to him how they had gone to see the Chief of Segu and said, "The Chief rejected the matter you sent us about. He prevented the gold being sent and said he would not give you any."

Then the Chief of Mande was angry, and he breathed heavily in his anger.

He called all his people to listen, saying, "Come, and hear the news."

When they had gathered he said to them "You know of the Chief of Segu. He has displeased me and it is because of this I have called you. Collect your beasts everyone of you." And so they all assembled on camels, horses and mules.

Then the Chief of Mande said "Cut down big trees and lay them on the ground"; and they did so.

Then he told the mounted men to jump over the trunks and they jumped over them until they split in half. They were kuka trees.

The Chief then called to them "Stand still," and they halted. He said, "As you went over the trees, go and do likewise to the Chief of Segu." But those who failed to go over the tree he sent back to their homes. And then two boys came forward from the crowd and they followed the company until they came to Segu. They razed Segu to the ground and they took prisoner the Chief. Of the two boys one was called Imoru and the other was called Bana'a.

Imoru the elder remained in Segu as Chief. He told Naba'a that he had received news of gold in a town called Gwona. "Go quickly," he said, "and come back quickly." This is the reason they were called Kagbanya. Naba'a went with his troops to Gwona; he looted the town and took much gold. Then he went to his town of Yagbum and stayed there. Now if any one does not know the meaning of Yagbum here it is. It is a big thing like a fort; for this reason it was called Yagbum.

After that Naba'a made a Jihad against Fula; he sacked the town of Fula, got much gold and then returned to Yagbum.

Version No. 2

The first king of Gonja was called Japa; he was also called Jarra. Now the King of Mande-Kabba, a great King, heard that gold was being found in the earth at Segu. So he sent a letter to the King of Segu saying that he wanted some of this gold. But the King of Segu refused to give him any so, the King of Mande-Kabba said he would come and take it. The King of Segu killed one of the messengers of the King of Mande-Kabba, but one made his escape and returned to the king. The king of Mande-Kabba marched on Segu but was prevented from reaching it by the river. So he made the people cut down trees for a bridge. They cut down many trees and made a bridge and the men of Mande-Kabba passed over it until at last the bridge gave way when only half the army had crossed. With those who crossed were the King of Mande-Kabba's sons, the first called Jarra Nabaha and another called Imoru. The army took Segu and found much loot and gold. Then a Mallam called Mohammedu Labayiru came to greet Nabaha and then returned to his house in company with another Mallam. He died before he reached his home and when the people told Nabaha that the Mallam was dead he sent money to make the funeral custom. This was the war of the King of Mande-Kabba against the King of Segu.

They were fighting, the men of Mande were in the sun while those of Segu were in the shade. Then the King of Mande said to Mallam Labayiru "See there is much sun, but our enemies are in the shade. Let us chase them out of the shade."

*Note:*I am indebted to Mr. Jack Goody from whose manuscript work on the "Ethnology of the Northern Territories of the Gold Coast" I obtained this translation.

Appendix XI
Bole Manuscript

Translated by Mallam Abudulai

Overpopulation and internecine warfare among the Nsauwa caused a section of them to leave Beawu. They first went to Segou, on the upper reachers of the Niger, and then in to Mendi. Later they moved East. The leaders in order of seniority were Namba, Wam, Lata, Lemu, Jaffa Mamfu, the last two full brothers, Manwura and Jakpa.

All these leaders came East from Mendi. At Palagu they fought their way to Baragu. They did not go to Bondouku bit via Ntereso to Wabili, then a big place, fourteen miles southwest of Bole. Thence they moved to Sakpa and it was this Chief who arranged that Wulasi, Mandare, Bole and Buanfo should make peace with the Gonjas. At Damba they all brought presents to Namba.

The Gonjas then went to Kapoasi.

At Kolon[1] they fought with the Abonifau (Nkoranza) when Namba was killed. Wam then conquered Kolon.

Nkoranza created trouble and Wam was killed.

Lata having driven off the Nkorana, returned to Kapoasi where he died.

Lemu then took over and fought and subdued the following countries North West of Bondouku: Palaga, Kong (Ilimini), Awuasu, Kongolu, Kwanyini and Samata. Going to Buna he was pacified with a house and cattle. Lemu died there and Jaffa succeeding him went to Bole where Mamfa died. It was circa A.D. 1760 in this year the Arab from Mecca who founded Larabanga came and was met. Jaffa went on towards Salaga. Janton, Parabe and Kakpande[2] make peace. Jaffa died at Vann[3] in the

---

1 Kolon may be Kawlaw, the name of the area round about Brumasi where a conflict with the Nkoranza could have taken place.

2 Janton, Parabe and Kakpande: The reference here is to the Mparaba Chiefs of Janton, Kakpande and Panshiaw. Parabe is undoubtedly intended for Mparaba and may refer by implication to Panchiavy-wura the senior of the three Mparaba Divisional Chiefs.

3 Vanna is Vano, a village West of Palbe.

same country. Manwura followed by subduing Nawuri, and Nchumuru where he died at Cheranhanteni.[4]

Jakpa, on succeeding, decided he had had enough of ward and determined to settle at Buipe where he returned. There he said "I am tired of fighting. All this country belongs to me. I will divide the country between my sons and my brother's sons."

To be Yabum (Paramount) Osumanu, Lata's son, Kagbawapeura, Osumanu refused the title stating he was not sufficiently powerful. But asked Jakpa to get on with the division. Jakpa then gave to:

Ewuretorma, Lata's son, Tuluwe
Burelanyon, Namba's son, Bole
Saaka, Namba's son, Kong
Darimani, Namba's son, Kandia
Yaya, Lemu's son, Kpembe
Seidu, Lemu's son, Kakpande
Yaya, Jaffa's son, Wasipe
Yaya, Manwura's son, Senyon
Seidu, Wam's son, Kusawgu

All had an equal chance to succeed to Yabum.

---

4 Cheranhanteni, East of Sabon Gida, near the Daka River.

Appendix XII
Kpembewura Soali's History

Translated from the Hausa of Mallam Mahama
by Lt. Col. A. Duncan Johnstone

Origin of the Race called Kagbanya or Gonja

Now this is the thing which happened amongst all the Chiefs and how
the Chief of Kombi became the head Chief. And in the days of our forefathers it came to pass that the Chief of Yabum called Ndewura Jakpa he
was over all the Chiefs. Now Ndewura Jakpa was the leader of all the
Gonjawa, the Chumbulawa (Nchuwurus), and the Nawurawa (Nawuris).
He came out of Mende (Mandingo), to the West, which is called the
country of the Wangara (Mandingo speaking race). He came with his
people the Gonjas, Nawuris and Nchumurus. He came first to the
country of the Tonawa, that is to say Ashanti. He came not with war, but
in peace.

So the Tonawa followed him, for he Ndewura Jakpa was a strong
man.

Now Osei Tutu reigned over the Tonawa and he was a great Chief.
And he was the King of Coomassie. Now Osei Tutu went on a journey
to Yabum to see the Chief Ndewura Jakpa. And when he came he said
unto him "I have come greet you not for nothing have I come to you."
And he said "I will be your war Chief I will command your soldiers." "I
will follow Allah and I and my people will follow you."

Then Osei Tutu took his younger sister who was called Adjua and he
gave her in marriage to the Chief Ndewura Jakpa.

Then it came to pass that Adjua bore a son to Ndewura Jakpa and
they called him Mahama.

Then Osei Tutu led the men of Ndewura Jakpa and they fought with
the Dagombas.

Now when the hear of Ndewura Jakpa turned from war, he Osei
Tutu came to him and said unto him 'Chief, behold the wars are finished
and the country is now cold. Therefore do I salute you and seek to return
to the forest where I may rest. There I will make my farms. I am now
old, moreover the Dagombas are no longer powerful." And Ndewura

Jakpa said unto him "Go in peace, I salute you." And it came to pass that Osei Tutu returned to the forest and Ndewura Jakpa reigned at Yabum.

So when Ndewura Jakpa was old and full of years he took the chair of the government and gave it to his son Ibrahima. Now Ibrahima was the younger, and Mahama the elder brother. Moreover Adjua, the mother of mahama grew angry and she said unto Ndewura Jakpa

> Behold I Adjua with my brother, the Chief Osei Tutu did help you in your wars. Did we not trouble ourselves with your affairs until you became strong? Now behold you have taken the stool of government and given it unto Ibrahima. But to Mahama the elder have you given nothing. Because of this thing which you have wrought, I will be your wife no longer. For I will depart and go to my brother Osei Tutu and I will stay with him, I and my son Mahama.

So she went together with her son, Mahama and left Ibrahima, Chief of Yabum.

Now the Chief Ndewura Jakpa died and Ibrahima reigned alone at Yabum. And he took counsel with himself and grew troubled. And he gathered together all his Chiefs and said unto them

> Behold I am but a boy, and I wish to do that is right for my brother Mahama. For am not I the younger brother, and I am Chief of Yabum. Therefore harken unto my commands. For each year and for all year ye shall look for slaves and sheep which ye will take unto Mahama my brother. Sashes for the waist of all colour also will ye take and give unto the uncle of Mahama called Osei Tutu.

Now these Cummerbunds or Sashes called "Kabichi" are worn to this day by the Gonjas, Nchumurus and Nawuris when they play and dance. And the fashion for wearing them is between the legs and round the waist to this day.

And it came to pass that when Osei Tutu died, Adjua, the sister of Osei Tutu took the stool of the government (Kujeran sarauanta) and gave it under her son Mahama. So Mahama reigned in Osei Tut's stead. Therefore to this day, this is the custom of the Tonawa (Ashantis). They only give the stool through the women, to the son of the Chief's sister. And so it came to pass that Mahama died, Chief of Ashanti and one followed him called Birri Sei.[1]

---

1 I can find no confirmation for these events. Adjua may have existed and been a wife of Ndewura Jakpa, but by no other account was he succeeded by his son Ibrahima and certainly there is no record of Mahama, Ibrahima's brother succeeding Osei Tutu as Asantehene. At one time, however, the Gonjas paid tribute to Ashanti and this may be an attempt to explain the fact.

So when news was brought to the Gonjas that the Chief Mahama was dead, they sent presents no longer. And the heart of Chief Birri Sei was wroth, until he sent messengers to the Gonjas to ask them concerning the slaves and the sheep and the sashes called "kabichi" which they were wont to sent Mahama. But the Gonjas answered and said "We give no longer."

So the messengers returned and told the Chief Birri Sei. Therefore was he angry and he sent his troops against the Gonjas. Now the name of the general who led the troops was Asamoa.[2] And he fought the Gonjas at Yabum. Now amongst the troops of the Gonjas were the Chumbulawa (Nchumurus). And the Chief of Alfaire was there also with his people the Nawurawa (Nawuris). For they were all one people and followed Ndewura Jakpa from Mandingo. Now the Ashantis defeated the Gonjas and the Gonjas did homage to the Ashantis. And they carried on the war until they reached the country of the Dagombas. And they conquered the Dagombas.

But the Ashantis did not enslave the Gonjas, the Nchumurus or the Nawuries but left them in their own country. And they were one people. And Asamoa returned with his people to the forest.

The conquest of the land by Ndewura Jakpa.
The Konkombas driven from the land now called Alfaire.
The division of the land.

Relationship between the Nawuris and the Gonjas

Now the Chief Ndewura Jakpa in his wars came to the lands of Kombi and took them. And he took his brother called Bori and set him over Kombi.

Now the people over the river (Dakar) were Konkombas, they lived on the land of Alfaire which was Konkomba. And when they heard of the name Ndewura Jakpa they were much afraid. And they left their lands and ran away. Then Ndewura Jakpa took his son and set him over the land of the Konkombas and he gave to it the name of Alfaire. Now the name of the son of Ndewura Jakpa of Alfaire was Djoro.

And Ndewura Jakpa divided the lands which he had conquered. to his brother Bori he gave Kombi. To his son Djoro he gave Alfaire. To the Chief of Kuli[3] he gave a piece of land, to the Chief of Tuluwi and to the Chief of Bunbung, and to the Chief of Alfaire, he gave land. And these Chiefs served the Chief of Kombi.

---

2 Probably Asamoah Nkwanta a famous Ashanti General who also figures in the History of the Mo people as recorded in a paper give to me by Bamboikoro in 1952.

3 Kilibiwura.

And Ndewura Jakpa divided the people who had come with him and the Nawuries he gave unto his son Djoro, Chief of Alfaire to serve him. And Bori, Chief of Kombi Chief of Gonjas reigned at Kombi.

Now this was the relationship between the Gonjas and the Nawuris. Now the country given to Djoro by Ndewura Jakpa was very big and as there was much space in it many people came to settle there. They begged Djoro and he gave them land. And they hunted the elephant, and they took ivory, out of two tusks they gave one to Djoro Chief of Alfaire. And this is their custom to the present day. They hunted the hippopotamus and they took a leg which they cut into seventy pieces to give to Djoro. This they did always.

And the name of the Chief of Alfaire went abroad until all men knew him, and he was called Kanakulaiwura which is to say, Chief of spearing hippo meat. Thus did he receive tribute.

> The Nchumurus and the Gonjas. Their relationship. Concerning the pagans of Kratchi their connection with the Gonjas and their fetish Dente or Late. Now the Nchumurus were divided and called Banda and Kakanki. How the Kakanki were late in arriving and *how Ndewura Jakpa gave them to Sunbung.*

Let us relate to you the story of the Nchumurus and how they are related to the Gonjas.

The Chief of Yabum, Ndewuar Jakpa he came also with the Nchumuru. He brought the Gonjas, the Nawuris, the Nchumurus out of Mande (Mandingo). And when he was coming, some of the Nchumurus delayed behind on the road, but some followed Ndewura Jakpa. Now to those who came first with Ndewura Jakpa gave he the lands of Banda where they dwell to this day. Now the people of Banda are blacksmiths.

Now when Ndewura Jakpa had founded the town of Yabum he came to Kombi. And those of the Nchumurus who had delayed behind on the road came to Yabum and they followed Ndewura Jakpa to Kombi. Now those of the Nchumurus who came first were called Banda and those who came after were called Kakanki. Now when the Chief Ndewura Jakpa had divided the lands of Kombi and Alfaire he said to the Kakanki. "Because you have delayed in coming, those who came first with me are the big people." So he took them and gave them to the Chief of Sumbung and they peopled the land. Now this was the connection between the Gonjas and the Kakanki (Nchumurus).

Concerning the pagans of Kratchi who follow the fetish called Late (Dente).[4]

---

4 Krachi Dente is a very popular Fetish in the Sumbung and Alfai Sub-Divisions of Kpembe.

Now Ndewura Jakpa conquered the land, the pagans of Kratchi came to him and followed him. And it came to pass that when Ndewura Jakpa had made an end of dividing the lands he returned to Yabum. And his brother Bori reigned at Kombi. Then did the pagans of Kratchi come again to Bori Chief of Kombi and saluted him. They said unto him "Behold there is a great fetish in our country called Late (Dente). Therefore we are come to tell you peradventure you may wish to have dealings with it." And the Chief of Kombi answered

> Yes I will do this. Return you to the fetish and serve it. But bring me the news which you hear from the fetish, all news concerning my kingdom. I do not want you for slaves, but only that you may assist me with your fetish. But the things which you require to propitiate the fetish, cattle and sheep. You must come to me and receive them. When my country is dry and there is no rain, intercede with the fetish that it may bring the rain. When our women do not bear children help them to do so, that we may grow big. This is the thing I wish done.

So spoke Bori Chief of Kombi. Now this was the connection between the Gonjas and the pagans of Kratchi.

> Gonjas, Nawuris, Nchumurus are people with one language. How they forgot their language. How the People of Banda still speak it. The sons of Ndewura Jakpa. *His reign and death in the year of the Hegira 1093.*

Now this was how our ancestor the Chief Ndewura Jakpa left the country of Mende and set up his kingdom. And the people who followed him were the Gonjas, the Nawuris, the Bandas and the Kakankis who are Nchumurus. And they were one people, with one language.

And the Gonjas, the Nawuris and the Nchumurus forgot the language of their forefathers. But the Bandas speak it to this day.[5] And all these people came from Mende which is called Wangara (Mandingo).

And Ndewura Jakpa was a great Chief and he conquered much country. And his son Mahama ruled the Tonawa (Ashanti). And his son Ibrahima ruled at Yabum. And his son Djore ruled in Alfaire. And his brother Bori ruled at Kombi. And the Chief of Sunbung, and Tuluwe and Kuli followed him. To them also he gave land. And Ndewura Jakpa he ruled over all.

---

5 The Lighi of Banda are Mande speakers.

And it came to pass that Ndewura Jakpa grew old and he died. And the year of his death was the 1093rd[6] year of the Hegira. And he ruled for forty-four years until he grew old. And he took the chair of government and gave it to his son Ibrahima.

And Ibrahima ruled for six years when Ndewura Jakpa died. And he died in the 1093rd year of the Hegira. And Ibrahima ruled again for sixteen years after the death of his father Ndewura Jakpa. And he ruled altogether for twenty-two years until he died. From that day to this it is 1900 years. During the reign of Ibrahima was a war which lasted for one year.

---

6 The same date as that given in Kanakulaiwura's Ms. 1681/82. This consistency of chronology extends to Ibrahima's reign who may well be one and the same as So'ara, 1675/76–1696/97 in this Ms., in the Kanakaulaiwura's Ms, his dates are 1675/76– 1697/98.

APPENDIX XIII
BOOKS AND PERSONS CONSULTED
BIBLIOGRAPHY

Published Works

W.W. Claridge *A History of the Gold Coast and Ashanti.*
W.E.P. Ward   *A History of the Gold Coast.*
F.O. Fuller   *A Vanished Dynasty—Ashanti.*
E.P. Tamakloe *A Brief History of the Dagbamba People.*
J. Withers Gill *A Short History of Salaga.*
A.S. Tritton   *Islam.*
H.A.R. Gibb   *Mohammedanism.*
G. Parrinder   *West African Psychology.*

Unpublished Works and Records

J. Goody   "Ethnology of the Northern Territories of
               the Gold Coast."

Bole District Records.
Salaga District Records.

Persons

Buipewura and elders.
Kpembewura and elders.
Wasipewura and elders.
Bolewura and elders.
Kusawguwura
Senyonwura
Damongowura
Mangpawura
Choriwura
Elders of Debrewura and Kawlawura
Sakpawura
Seripewura
Soomia'wuriche with Ewuriches of Bole Division
Karanzanwura Osumanu
Kanakulaiwura
Kanyasiwura
Sumbunwura
Kilibiwura
Panshiawwura

Jantonwura
Kakpandewura
Buipe Liman and Mallams
Kpembe Liman
Bole Liman
Mallam Basabte Watera
Kotia Ligbi
Salia Kurabari
Dabo

Besides the above, I am indebted to many others for their help.

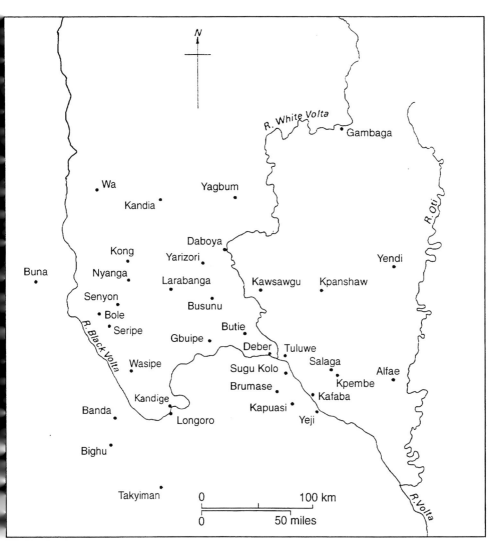

Map 3. Principal towns and villages of Gonja.

Gonja Traditional and Customary Practice and Procedure in Chieftaincy Matters Since 1923

Compiled by Osafroadu Amankwatia
Counsel to the Northern Regional House of Chiefs

Tamale

Chieftaincy Matters: Areas of Research into Gonja Traditional Area (Gbanya Kingdom)

The Kingdom of (Gbanya) Gonja is believed to have been founded in the sixteenth century by famous horsemen known as Mande, who must have originated from the North-Western part of Ghana, and possibly of the Mambara origin near Techiman (Bonso Mansu) in the Brong-Ahafo Region of Ghana.

Ndewura Jakpa is also believed to have been a powerful chief of his time from whom the entire royal families of the Gonja peoples trace their ancestral origins through the paternal lineage. Ndewura Jakpa was highly assisted by powerful Imams of his time, particularly with Sakpare in his territorial conquest against Mamprusi, Dagomba and Nanumba states and extended his dynasty across the Volta Rivers into what is now known as the Northern Region of Ghana, of which Gonja forms part administratively as one of the four main autonomous and traditional constituent areas within the Northern Regional House of Chiefs.

The official title of the Gonja Traditional Paramountcy is the Yabumwura, and the traditional and political history of the Gonjas have it that the Paramount chiefly office of Yabumwura should at all times be filled in rotation by the heads of the various territorial divisions of Gonja, who claim as of right to be descended patrilineally from Ndewura Jakpa, and this system of inheritance is the "gates" or families of chiefly office up to the paramountcy in Gonja Traditional Area.

Before this period the various divisions of Gonja have always been autonomous and it was the British Colonial Government who contemplated a union for the whole of Gonja on the 10th day of February, 1923.

The Nawuris have been causing troubles since the early 1940s and have been demanding independence from Gonja overlordship. The Nawuris were brought and planted in the Alfai (Kpandae) area by the Gonjas under Ndewura Jakpa as mercenaries. They therefore were not on good terms with Gonjas and this was the result of their disagreements with the Gonjas, they therefore decided to vote in the 1955 Plebescite for the Togo Unification and the Dixon Commission was appointed to investigate their claims for independence.

However, the Nawuris are today a minority group in the Kpandae area of Gonja where the Konkombas, Basaris, Kotokolis, Chemhas and other tribes have settled and these tribes accept the Gonjas as their overlords (Chiefs) and are now law abiding.

The old Gbanya Kingdom had disintegrated before the coming of the Europeans, owing to tribal disagreements, internecine slave trade and slave raiding. During the period of peace following the British occupation and administration of this country Gbanya had remained divided, one portion lying in the Tamale administrative district, one portion divided between the districts of Eastern Gonja and Western Gonja, and yet another portion which was up to the outbreak of the great War I, under the Germans in Togoland was administered by a District Commissioner at Krachi. Although the chiefs of Gonja still give their customary allegiance to the Yabumwura both Yabumwura and the chiefs had lost much of their ancient power and had indeed become nothing more than figure-heads thereby leaving the administration of their country almost entirely in the hands of the District Commissioners appointed by the foreign powers.

It was felt that the time had come to ratify this and as a first measure the British Government had decided that Gbanya should be reunited under the hereditary Paramount chief in the person of Yabumwura.

It was further proposed that the chiefs should be allowed to exercise some measure of their old jurisdiction and to settle disputes and other criminal and civil cases in their own states by the customary law and usage.

To this end, political officers such as commissioners must be prepared to take the onus of administration of Gbanya.

The Commissioner of the Southern Province of the Northern Territories pointed out that before any plan of administration could be drawn up, the proper order of precedence of Chiefs, Divisional Chiefs and Councillors according to their ancient custom and tradition should be clearly defined by the Chiefs themselves; and so also was the question of the order of seniority which must also be known and the Chiefs and elders were the qualified people to declare their status.

The Commissioner of the Southern Province further reminded the Yabumwura and the Chiefs that the fact that they were to be allowed to exercise some of their former powers did not mean that they were to become independent of the British Colonial Government; but that they were to take more active part in helping the Government as an integral part of the Government in administering Gbanya's traditional area.

The Yabumwura after the meeting with the Commissioner of the Southern Province, then rose, his Dogte (Linguist) with his silver staff in his right hand and his Mezembewura (Chief archer) on his left side thanked the Commissioner and asked for a further time, to call all his chief elders together for a discussion and for a decision on the whole matter, the Commissioner had put before him to decide as to the correct hereditary order of seniority of Chiefs as well as the status of the various chiefs within the Gonja Traditional area.

At the meeting of the Chiefs on the 17th to 19th day of May, 1930 when all the chiefs of Gonja assembled, it was discovered that there was no order of sitting at the palaver with the exception of Yabumwura and his elders. This was explained by the fact that it has been many years since the chiefs of Gonja assembled together and therefore the order of sitting had been forgotten or disregarded.

However, at all palavers the Yabumwura and his entourage sit in the centre slightly in advance of the other chiefs with his own personal councillors around him and the remaining other chiefs group themselves on each side of the Yabumwura.

Custom has it that the Buipewura who was then a very old man and was not expected to be able to attend the meeting caused great astonishment to everybody there by his presence. Custom again has it that the Buipewura and the Yabumwura are not to see each other therefore when the Buipewura rose to speak at the meeting a large cloth was held on his left side so that he and the Yabumwura could not look at one and the other. At this meeting, which is officially known as the "Enquiry into the Constitution and Organisation of the Gbanya Kingdom," was the actual starting point of the unification of the people of the Gonja Traditional area as it is today. It was at this meeting that the chiefs settled the following points for the administration of Gonja:

a. List of Precedence of Divisional Chiefs, senior chiefs, and State Councillors.
b. List of Councillors forming the executive council of the Gonja Traditional area.
c. List of Chiefs forming the Gonja Legislative Council.
d. List of Divisional Chiefs eligible for election to the Skin of Yabum (Kawul Puti).
e. Rules of succession and list of those eligible for election to the Kawul of the Divisions as Divisional Chiefs.

To this end all the above-named Divisions or arms of the Gonja government was later complied with, and when the chiefs assembled again on Monday the 19th day of May, 1930, the said arrangements which were duly put down in writing was announced and read and interpreted by the Nsogowura (Head Dogta or Linguist) and acclaimed by the assembled chiefs. These documents having been duly verified by Mr. Duncan Johnson the then Commissioner of the Southern Province of the Northern

Territories, A.W. Cardinal the then District Commissioner, Western Gonja, and Captain E.A. Bura O.B.E., the then District Commissioner of Eastern Gonja requested the Yabumwura, the Divisional Chiefs, Sub-chiefs and the Councillors to confirm their acceptance of the conditions of the documents duly established to be signed by all of them by thumbprinting the document to be the binding law of the Gonja State.

To conclude the unity the Commissioner of the Southern Province of the Northern Territories asked the Divisional Chiefs, sub-chiefs, councillors and the elders and in fact all the Gonja people if they were willing to sign a document setting forth their desire to serve the Yabumwura as their overlord and Paramount chief of the united Gonja State. To this end, they unanimously agreed and signing/thumbprinting the document as their deed and act in the presence of the Commissioner.

List of Precedence of Divisional Chiefs

This list has little or nothing to do with the order of meeting at a palaver and the curious thing about it is that comparatively small chiefs take precedence over divisional chiefs. This may be so because of the pre-rogative right of the Yabumwura to appoint some of the smaller chiefs as his direct elders and therefore take precedence over the divisional chiefs.

List of Councillors Forming the Executive Council of the Gonja State

This council consists of six divisional chiefs under the Presidency of the Kagbapewura, who represents the Buipewura.

These councillors are all senior in rank. The six divisional chiefs from whom the Yabumwura is chosen have certain privileges which they enjoy by themselves, such as the paying of tribute in the olden days, and their villages having the right of sanctuary for anyone fleeing from the Yabumwura or any of the chiefs. When the whole of the Gbanya meet to elect the Yabumwura this Council takes part and conveys the decision to the Buipewura.

List of Chiefs Forming the Legislative Council of Gonja

This council is composed of the executive council mentioned above and the divisional chiefs within the Gonja Traditional Area and consists of the Divisional chiefs and the Yabumwura's elders.

LIST OF DIVISIONAL CHIEFS ELIGIBLE FOR ELECTION TO THE KAWUL PUTI (SKIN CUSHION OF YABUN)

This list was furnished by the Buipewura who confirms the election. It is to be observed that in all there are six divisional chiefs eligible but out of the present list only three are in fact eligible to be put up for election, namely; Kusawgu, Tuluwe and Kpembe.

Of the remaining three chiefs the skin of Kung was in abeyance the last chief having been claimed and his people almost annihilated by the Bole people about 1895/96 when Kung joined the forces of Samori and fought against the other Kagbanya. The villages in the Kingdom or division were then divided, some being put under Bole and the remainder went direct under Yabun.

The Yabumwura stated in the Conference that he contemplated re-creating a divisional court for the villages which all serve him directly.

The Kande division was also non-existent and its villages lie over the border in the Wa district.

It was ascertained that at the Gbanya Conference held at Yapei in February, 1923 the chief of Templuma near Ducie in the Wa district, who was the heir to the Kande chiefdom wished to attend the Conference of 1923 but he was forbidden to do so by the Chief Commissioner of Northern Territories.

In the case of Bole it was discovered that the then Chief of Bole was not eligible for election to Kawul Puti for the reason that the chief ought to be chosen from the Villages of Mandare, Wulawi or Juntillipe and the holder of the office was appointed from Tuna by the then District Commissioner, Western Gonja, Mr. Bruce Hall, in defiance of native custom and against the wishes of the Yabumwura. This irregularity was afterwards excused by the Yabumwura when the District Commissioner informed him that he wanted a strong man to be the chief of Bole.

The remaining divisional chief of Wasipe (Daboya) had also been found to have been wrongly appointed by the then District Commissioner of Tamale who deposed the old chief for misconduct in 1929 and appointed the present occupant who is outside the line of succession and therefore could never be elected by the Yabumwura. The Yabumwura later complained of the chief of Wasipe and wished to depose him forwith as the Wasipewura had never come to salute him the Yabumwura or informed him that he was on the skin of Wasipe (Daboya).

The Yabumwura wished to put the Wasipe skin into the keeping of the Yasoriwura for the time being but he was advised by the Commissioner, Southern Province not to take that action but to hold the matter over until the end of the conference.

NATIVE TRIBUNALS

At the later stages of the Conference of 1930, discussions were held concerning the constitution of native tribunals and their jurisdictions. It appeared that there were three district grades of recognised tribunals all of which were based on the village unit and their jurisdiction was mainly of an arbitrative nature and therefore had no executive power. The second grade of tribunals comprised what may be now termed the divisional courts as they were presided over by the Wura of each division. The third grade consists of courts lower than the divisional courts and presided over by the Wuras of the various sub-divisions. From these third grade courts one could appeal in the first instance to the divisional courts and from there to the first grade court of the Yabumwura.

As time went on, it was discovered that there was one court of Senyo which was of a different nature to all the other courts. It was presided over by the Senyowura and its members were exclusively religious leaders known as Kasawulewura. That is to say Tindana or as they are known in Dagbani, Dakpema, the priest of the Land.

This Senyo Court was mostly concerned with land cases and matters affecting the observance and reverence owed to the spirits of the land. For this reason, it was decided to classify it as a native court in so much as its members belong exclusively to a religious sect of Dagomba as opposed to the feudal courts presided over and composed mainly of the Wuras and other alien ruling races of Gonja.

It was again agreed that the Senyowura was to be the head of all the land priests in Western Gonja and also a customary legal adviser to the Yabumwura in all land cases. He also had his seat in the appellate court of the Yabumwura.

The outstanding feature of the divisional and sub-divisional courts was that in many cases they contained amongst their members the following:

> The Liman who presumably advised the courts in cases where the participants are Moslems and the Kajemowura, the village head was represented by the indigenous people being the Kasawulewura or Tindena, meaning "The owner of the land" or rather the senior priest of the land and the Wuriche, chiefs who are chiefs' daughters and who have jurisdiction over the women folk of Gonja.

On the final resumption of the Conference the Yabumwura brought up the following matters for further discussion:

> a. The friction between the Kanakulaiwura and the Sunbungwura as to the order of their precedence.

b. The appointment of the chief of Wasipe.

c. The construction of road from Bole to Yapei.

d. A new district headquarters to be posted at Yapei.

Finally the Commissioner, Southern Province, agreed that this was true as regards the Wasipewura but pointed out that probably, confusion had been caused by the fact the Daboya was at that time in the Western Dagomba district and therefore the Wasipe chief might not have been able to go to pay his respects to the Yabumwura. The Commissioner further said that if that was all the case against the Wasipewura, who had a good record, it would be a pity to tarnish the Yabumwura's newly restored power by putting the Wasipewura off the skin.

The Buipewura then advised the Yabumwura to accept the advice given to him by the Commissioner, Southern Province.

Then followed the question about the friction between the Kanakulaiwura of Alfaire (Togoland) and the Sungbungwura of Salaga both in the line of succession to the Kpembe skin and therefore to the Kawul Puti.

The Yabumwura then referred to the question of seniority between Kanakulaiwura and Sungbung and declared the Kanakulaiwura to take precedence of Sungbung.

GONJA ROYAL MAUSOLEUM

The Buipewura, who is not a Divisional Chief is most revered, honoured and highly respected in the Gonja Traditional area. The reason being that he is the customary and traditional father of the Yabumwura, and therefore in rank Buipewura is placed on the same level as the Yabumwura.

His town is Buipe, where the royal mausoleum for the Yabumwura's father is situated and the Buipewura is the caretaker of the royal Burial Grounds.

It will be noticed that the Buipewura is the Traditional President of the Gonja State Executive Council of seven members composed of Divisional Chiefs. On the decease of a reigning Yabumwura they have to choose a new Paramount Chief from among the seven members of the State Executive Council, over which the Kagbapewura presides in the absence of the Buipewura.

When the nomination of the Yabumwura elect is accomplished the said Council conveys the decision to the Buipewura by the practice and usage of the Gonjas. The Buipewura has the traditional right to confirm the election of Yabumwura but he the Buipewura and the Yabumwura are by custom never to meet face to face after the installation of the Yabumwura.

This taboo has once been broken when the Buipewura, who was then old and blind, caused great astonishment when he unavoidably attended the Yapei Enquiry into the Constitution and organisation of the Gbanya Kingdom, held in 1930.

At this meeting he was careful to sit as far away as possible from the Yabumwura and when he rose to give evidence, even though blind, a large cloth was held on his left side so that the Yabumwura could not look at him nor could they see each other throughout the Conference.

The reason for this taboo is that they are by custom to pay homage and give reverence to each other on equal terms and conditions; but to avoid these, custom prohibits them to meet in person on any occasion. The custom continues to the present day in Gonja.

A. DEATH OF A YABUMWURA (BURIAL OF A YABUMWURA)

1.
   a. When the Yabumwura dies it is the duty and responsibility of the people of Jentilipe to cut the buttress of a silk-cotton tree in Nyanga and carve it into a bier on which the body is carried to Mankuma for burial after the linguists have performed their customary rites on the corpse.
   b. It is the duty and responsibility of the blacksmiths in Sawla to forge nails for nailing to the bier to keep the body in position and make it easy for its conveyance to Mankuma.
   c. It is the duty and responsibility of the Nlusah (diviners) of the Nangbewura of Mankuma to dig the grave and bury the deceased Yabumwura. On the death of Yabumwura the Nlusah are the first to be informed and they must perform certain secret customary rites before the funeral of the deceased Yabumwura is formally announced.

2. **Funeral Announcement** On the death of a Yabumwura, the Sonyonwura sends the deceased Yabumwura's horse, unsaddled, together with his staff and sandals to the Gbipewura (Buipewura) to announce the death of the Paramount Chief. On the receipt of the formal notification the Gbipewura will inform the Kagbapewura of the Yabumwura's death.

3. **Regency**

   a. The Sonyonwura, according to custom, becomes the acting Head of State on the death of Yabumwura and he administers the affairs of the State until a new Yabumwura is selected.
   b. Two *Wurkongs* (Regents), *Wurkong-nyin* and *Wurkong-che* (male regent and female regent who must be the son and the daughter of the late Yabumwura) are appointed and installed but their main functions are in connection with the funeral. The *Wurkong-*

nyin is, however, given the reverence that is due to the Yabumwura.

c. The male *Wurkong* is discharged after the performance of the
twelfth day funeral and the female *Wurkong* is discharged
together with the widows after a period of five months.

4. **Funeral Performance (Third-day Funeral)** The Bolewura, being the
nearest Divisional Chief to the Paramount chief, is responsible for the
performance of the third day funeral.

5. **Seventh Day Funeral** The members of the deceased family are
responsible for the performance of the seventh day funeral but they
cannot perform the funeral unless all the Divisional Chiefs and elders are
present.

6. **Twelfth Day Funeral** The twelfth day funeral is performed by the
Yabumwura elect before his installation. This is to enable the late chief's
widows, who have chosen to wear white cloths during their widowhood,
to leave the town after their one week confinement as the new Yabumwura must not, according to custom, see the widows of his predecessor
in their white mourning cloths.

C. Election of Yabumwura—Paramount Chief

7. After the performance of the seventh day funeral, at which all the
Divisional chiefs (Nkulongwura) and Elders (Binimu) are present, a meeting is held by the Divisional Chiefs (Nkulongwura) and Elders (Binimu)
who form the full Gonja Traditional Council for the Purpose of electing
a new Yabumwura.

8. **Presiding Member** The Sonyonwura, who becomes the Regent on
the death of a Yabumwura, and who administers the affairs of the Gonja
Traditional Area until a new Yabumwura is installed, presides at the
meeting.

9. **Members** The Divisional Chiefs who are members of the electoral
body and from whose membership a candidate is selected are: 1.
Wasipewura, 2. Kpembewura, 3. Bolewura, 4. Tuluwewura, and 5. Kusawguwura.

10. **The Elders (Binimu) who are members of the electoral body are:**
1. Sonyonwura, 2. Damongowura, 3. Debrewura, 4. Mankpangwura, 5.
Choriwura, and 6. Kulawwura.

11. Nomination of Candidates The Sonyonwura will call for the nomination of candidates when the meeting is formally opened. In the nomination of candidates care is taken to see that the Divisional Chief who is next in the order of rotation among the five Divisional Chiefs who are eligible to the Yabum Paramountcy is nominated. Only under special circumstances would a Division be bypassed in favour of another.

12. After nomination, the claims of contestants are discussed and generally a consensus is reached and the agreed candidate's name is announced to the Sonyonwura. Voting, i.e. teaming up behind candidates, becomes necessary only when no agreement can be reached on one acceptable candidate.

13. The Sonyonwura will send a Dogte (Linguist) to the Gbipewura to report to him the name of the Divisional Chief who has been elected as the new Yabumwura. The Buipewura's duty would be to give the appointment his formal approval and he has no right to reject the candidate.

14. The Sonyonwura will also report, by letter, to the nearest District Administrative Officer, who is the Government's representative in the area, the results of the election for the information of Government and for recognition to be accorded him and for his name to be published in the Government Gazette.

15. After his election, the Yabumwura elect will be given the responsibility of performing the Twelfth Day Funeral of the late Yabumwura.

16. The Yabumwura elect will inform the Buipewura of the suitable date he had chosen for his installation. The installation should take place early in order not to cause inconveniences to the Divisional Chiefs and the Elders who must return to their homes to carry on with the administration of their respective areas.

17. When a date had been agreed, the Buipewura will ask the Kagbapewura to go and install the new chief.

18. The amount to be paid to the Kagbapewura by the Yabumwura elect is negotiated between the two persons when the former arrives.

19. When the Yabumwura is installed he goes into confinement for seven days, at the end of which he appears in public. He makes his policy statement and, thereafter, the Divisional Chiefs and the Elders will beg leave of him to return to their respective homes.

INVENTORY OF SKIN PROPERTIES

20. On the election of a new Yabumwura the head of the late chief's family will see that the skin properties are handed over to the Sonyonwura and it is the duty of the head of the late chief's family to witness the checking and handing over of the skin properties. If any is missing it will be the head of the family who is held responsible.

21. The Sonyonwura will in turn hand the skin properties over to the Yabumwura elect in the presence of the senior members of his (the Yabumwura elect) family and those of the late Yabumwura's family.

DIVISIONAL CHIEFS AND YABUMWURA'S ELDERS

22. In the case of the Divisional Chiefs and the Elders (Binimu) who are Councillors to the Yabumwura, the head of the late chief's family will hand over the skins and skin properties to the customary regent when a new chief is elected and see to it that the skin properties are checked and found to be correct. He will be responsible for any missing articles, which he will have to replace, if they are replaceable.

23. The Regent will in turn hand them over to the new chief elect in the presence of the senior members of his family and those of the late chief's family.

24. In Kpembe the regent is always the Kilibuwura who presides over the meeting of the King-makers and elders who decide on whom the next Kpembe skin should fall.

25. Movable and Immovable Self Acquired Properties Besides the skins and other skin properties, all the other properties are personal properties of the deceased chief and these are inherited by the members of the deceased chief's family.

26. Customarily the deskinment of the Yabumwura or any chief in Gonja is unknown and therefore uncustomary. Deskinment was introduced by the British officials who administered the areas and a chief was removed only on a complaint made against him by the District Commissioner as agent of the Central Government. If any chief was disliked by his people the only way of getting rid of him was to fight and defeat him, and thereby get rid of him.

27. A chief shall be suspended only if it is proved that he has committed felony.

28. A person can only be disqualified from occupying the Yabum or any other skins if it is proved that he:

    i. is in any way deformed especially by the loss of the big toe which can prevent him from wearing sandals.

    ii. has committed felony.

    iii. has been to prison for a criminal offence involving dishonesty.

    iv. is deaf

    v. is blind (blindness whilst on the skins is exempted).

    vi. is of unsound mind.

29. Nkulongwura and Binimu—Election and Appointment of Divisional Chiefs and Elders The filling of vacant skins in Gonja is generally by rotation between two or more families known as *Mbuna* (gates) existing in the various Divisions of the Gonja Traditional area.

30.

    a. After the "Third or Seventh Day Funeral" of a deceased Divisional chief the gate chiefs of the Division and the elders must call on the Yabumwura who will elect them a new chief from the next gate. Vacancy must be filled in rotation and the skin must go to the next gate in succession as a matter of course.

    b. After the "Third or Seventh Day Funeral" of a deceased Buipewura the Kortey and Sapkare gates will meet, get the right candidate, and must call on the Yabumwura to inform him of the candidate and seek for his approval.

        The presiding Chief is always the person who by custom becomes the regent administering the affairs of the Division whenever the skins become vacant resulting from the death of the Divisional Chief.

31. If, on the other hand, the Yabumwura and his skin makers elected chief is disputed, the Traditional Council shall be summoned to determine the matter.

32. When the dispute is settled, and the Yabumwura is satisfied, he shall give formal approval to the elected candidate, or the person to whom judgement is given.

33. No fixed amounts are paid to the Yabumwura as "thanks kola" (*Kapushe*) for appointing, or approving the appointment of, a chief. A candidate shall pay any amount he is able to offer, and in addition to provide drink to the Yabumwura's elders and Councillors to seal his appointment.

34. The Divisional Chief, or Elder, elect shall return to his home town with his sub-chiefs and elders and he may appoint a convenient date for his installation. The installation shall be done according to the custom of the area.

35. It shall be unconstitutional to bypass a family whose turn it is to fill a vacant skin and appoint another to supersede it, as this results in disunity among the royals and leads to trouble in the area. It shall be unconstitutional to allow pecuniary considerations to influence the appointment of wrong persons to vacant skins.

36. The Yabumwura's Nsuawura is appointed by the Yabumwura. Traditionally no one bypasses the Nsuawura to call on the Yabumwura.

D. APPOINTMENT OF SUB-CHIEFS

37. Sub-chiefs are and shall continue to be appointed by the Divisional Chiefs (Nkulongwura) and elders (Binimu) in whose area of jurisdiction they are.

38. Before the appointment of a sub-chief the Divisional chief will consult with the members of the families eligible to the chiefship and a member of the family next in order of rotation shall be appointed.

Appointment of Sub-Chiefs in the Kpembe Division

a) The Kpembewura appoints the following sub-chiefs who have areas covering a number of villages under their jurisdiction;

   a. Kilibuwura
   b. Kafabawura
   c. Singbingwura
   d. Kanyasewura
   e. Kanakulaiwura
   f. Kawosewura

b) In addition to these sub-chiefs, the Kpembewura also appoints his elders and the Leppowura who is his aide-de-camp. The Leppo chiefship rotates with the Kpembe chiefship.

41. The six sub-chiefs mentioned above appoint the sub-chiefs and village headmen under their jurisdiction without any consultation whatsoever with the Kpembewura.

VILLAGE HEADMEN

42. Village Headmen are elected by their people and presented to the Divisional or Sub-chiefs or Elder under whose jurisdiction they are, for formal approval.

MBONGWURA

Mbongwura is appointed by the chief under whom he serves. The post of a Mbongwura (war Captain) is now honorary.

B'WURCHE (FEMALE CHIEFS)

Female Chiefs (B'wurche) are appointed by either

- *a.* the Yabumwura
- *b.* the Divisional chiefs and Elders (Nkulongwura) or
- *c.* sub-chiefs in whose areas of jurisdiction they are for, and for which offices the respective female chiefships exist.

DUTIES OF FEMALE CHIEFS

The duties of the female chiefs are to organise the women for any communal work, supervise the women in the preparing of food during the Damba and other festivals and prepare the ceremonial food (*Kusutu-dwe*) for the dead.

The female chief Iwurche is also consulted on major matters most especially on custom, by the chiefs and elders.

BICHE BI-BIBI CHIEFSHIPS

In the Bole Division, the sons of B'wurche (Female Chiefs) are, and will continue to be, entitled to the following chiefships:

- *i.* Seripe
- *ii.* Kulmasa
- *iii.* Maluwe
- *iv.* Kpankpansiri

An *Iwurche* (Female Chief) has nothing to do with the nomination of a chief as does the Akan Queen mother. The *Iwurche* need not be related to the chief appointing her, though she must be a member of the royal family and her father need not hold, nor have held, the office of a chief.

PRIVILEGES OF CHIEFS

In commutation of the occasional customary levies and court fees and fines, market fees, ferry tolls and import duty collected from strangers as well as the forced labour of the people to work on the chiefs' land on which chiefs depended for their upkeep in the past and which resources local councils now collect in rates and fees as their sources of revenue, chiefs are entitled to be paid salaries and allowances by the local councils covering their areas of jurisdiction.

Salaries will be paid only to Divisional Chiefs, Elders (Binimu) and other chiefs who are councillors to the Divisional Chiefs and Elders, who have lost to the local councils their sources of income.

Notwithstanding the payment of hunting fees paid by strangers to the local councils, all hunters including the inhabitants shall give to the chief in whose area of jurisdiction an animal is killed a hind leg of the game, and in addition give to the headman of the village one front leg of the game, according to Gonja custom.

One tusk, one ear, and one hind leg of any elephant killed is, according to custom, given to the Yabumwura or Divisional Chief, or Elder and councillor, in whose area the game was killed. Divisional Chiefs will, however, surrender such tributes to the Yabumwura.

The skins of lions and leopards killed in the Gonja Traditional area are, according to custom, given to the Divisional Chief or Enimu (Elder) in whose area the animal is killed and the Chief uses them as the skins of his office. It is uncustomary, and shall be an offence, for any chief to sell such skins when he receives them.

Notwithstanding the fact that fishing licences are taken out by strangers or any inhabitant from local authorities, any person who fishes in any reservoir, river, stream or other body of water in the area of authority of a chief shall give to such chief the customary Friday fish every week.

No person who has taken out a fishing licence from a local authority will be allowed to fish in lakes or ponds customarily belonging to a chief or a village headman or a village community except with the express permission of such chief, village headman, or village community.

Sylvan produce shall be collected according to the custom of the area and the wives and other relatives, daughters, of chiefs shall be treated in no way different from other women.

GONJA FESTIVALS

The Damba, Dongi Achan, Kuchunifol and Jintigi are annual festivals which the Gonja observe and these shall continue to be celebrated according to custom. The inhabitants shall continue to pay to their respective chiefs the tribute of cows, sheep, guinea fowls, flour, firewood, and any such tributes that are sanctioned by customary law existing in the various divisions of the traditional area, during the celebration of the respective festivals. Whether the modern conditions and the present economic changes of living will permit the continuance of this customary practice will be determined by the passage of time.

As the Damba festival is of major importance to all Divisional chiefs and Elders (Binimu) they shall all celebrate Damba in their homes, according to custom, and they may come in to the headquarters to help the Yabumwura celebrate his Damba occasionally only once in three years.

RELIGIOUS SACRIFICES

Chiefs shall give to their fetish priests within their respective areas who hold annual festivals at which sacrifices are made to the fetish, the animal, cow, sheep and/or fowl which they are, according to custom, expected to provide for the sacrifices.

58. Any modification of this custom, having regard to changed circumstances and modern requirements, and as a result of the chiefs losing much of their tributes and sources of revenue to local councils, shall be by mutual agreement between the chiefs concerned and their fetish priests.

PROTECTION OF SACRED GROVES

59. Sacred places, groves, cemeteries, fetishes and fetish houses are protected. Any person who violates any sacred place commits an offence and such sacrilege will be dealt with according to custom. Any person who unlawfully enters upon any land which is tabooed for the purposes of cultivation shall be required to perform the necessary sacrifices.

60. No person should put any other person in a fetish. Any fetish oath sworn for an unlawful purpose is hereby declared to be unlawful.

LAND

61. The land in Gonja remains the property of the community which is held in trust by the Chiefs on behalf of the people. All Gonja citizens are entitled to build houses or cultivate lands free of charge and they will not be required to pay any fees. The plots on which houses are built remain the property of the family and farm lands that are vacated for a period of two years shall revert to the general community and anyone desiring so to do is at liberty to cultivate such farm land.

MARRIAGE

62. Marriage customs among the various tribes in the Gonja Traditional area are so diverse that it is not easy to reduce them into writing. The different tribes and communities in the Gonja Traditional area shall continue to observe the customs governing their marriages as laid down by their ancestors. However, on no account should a girl be forced into marrying a person she does not like. However, marriage customs shall not remain static with the progress of time and civilisation.

PRIVATE BUSINESS OF CHIEFS

63. A chief should be free to be engaged in any profession or trade befitting the dignity of his office, but should call on all ceremonial occasions to take part in the annual festivals; provided the exigency of service, should he be a Public Officer or a civil servant, would allow him to do so in certain circumstances as the status of the Skins he occupies.

64. A Chief is at liberty to appear in any dress and to move about without an attendant (if he is outside his area of jurisdiction) except on formal and ceremonial occasions.

The Yabumwura nominates the Divisional Chiefs and the seven elders who are known as "Bugbonpo."

The Divisional Chiefs are: Wasipewura, Kpembewura, Bolewura, Tuluwewura, Kasawguwura, and Buipewura.

The Elders or "Bugbonpo" are also: Sonyonwura, Damongowura, Choriwura, Debrewura, Mankpanwura, Kulaw-wura, Kpansheguwura, and Busunuwura.

The Kpansheguwura and Busunuwura were made elders (Bugbonpo) at an emergency meeting of the Gonja Traditional Council to give final approval to the Gonja Customary law 29th–30th July, 1975.

A nominated person can therefore be installed as a Divisional Chief or Elder.

The deposition of a Yabumwura is quite unknown in the Gonja State, however, the Yabumwura, in consultation with the Traditional Council, can deskin any Divisional Chief or elder who acts contrary to the tradition and some laws of the country.

The Divisional Chiefs on the other hand are responsible for the enskinment and the deposition of the sub-chiefs within their respective divisional areas.

THE SKINMAKERS

In Gonja the Skinmakers are of different categories:

a. That of the Paramount are: the six divisional chiefs and seven elders (Bugbonpos)
b. That of the Divisional Chiefs and the elders of Bugbonpos is the Yabumwura, Paramount Chief in consultation with the elders, king-makers of the division concerned.
c. The Divisional Chiefs in consultation with their respective elders and sub-chief are also the skinmakers of their respective divisional areas.

In Gonja the skins which adopt patrilineal or matrilineal succession are known to the Royals. A person who lays claim to skins either by patrilineal or matrilineal succession cannot cross sides.

Patrilineal skins are more important than matrilineal ones and those who have equal opportunities to choose prefer the patrilineal skins. It is therefore very clear that inheritance is mainly patrilineal. Chieftaincy in Gonja rotates in the order of gates; it is not hereditary and the order of rotation is best known to the chiefs concerned.

The Queen mother has no role in the nomination, installation or deposition of chiefs. Her choice is never binding on the skinmakers.

The Paramount Chief prefers deskinment charges against any divisional chief or elder (Bugbonpo). A divisional chief can also prefer deskinment charges against any of his sub-chiefs.

Circumstances warranting the preference of deskinment charges against a chief are: constant refusal to honour the invitations of the Paramount or Divisional Chief, stealing, illegal possession of skin property. Defying government orders, disobeying the elders advice and contravening traditional taboos.

Stealing, selfishness, disobedience and pride are some of the main things that may call forth sanctions against a chief.

A chief automatically ceases to exercise the functions and powers of his office and accordingly draws allowances when his deskinment is made public by the entitled senior chief.

The Paramount Chief in consultation with the Traditional Council has the right to suspend any divisional chief for misbehaviour or conduct, disrespectful to the Paramount Chief/Traditional Council.

The appointment of a regent becomes necessary only a period of three days after the death of a chief.

In the case of the Paramount Chief, there should be two male regents.

    a. the traditional regent is the Sonyonwura, who is the most senior of the elders or "Bugbonpo";

    b. the second regent is elected from among the deceased's own brothers or sons.

Regency in Gonja is the same as for a substantive chief.

The regent wields all the powers of the chief and his term of tenure are limitless until the enskinment of a new chief.

The Yabumwura (President) who is the overall head of the Gonja state is immediately followed by his six elders or "Bugbonpo."

    b. the divisional chiefs: the Wasipewura, Kpembewura, Bolewura, Tuluwewura, Kusawguwura and Buipewura are next senior to the Yabumwura and his elders;

    c. the third group is the elected members of the Traditional Council.

The Gonja Traditional Council is of the following composition:

a.

    i.   the Yabumwura (President)

    ii.   the eight elders

    iii. the Yabumwura's Nsuawura

    iv. the six Divisional Chiefs and three sub-chiefs from each Divisional area

Besides the three (3) elected chiefs from each Divisional area, who are not permanent, the Traditional Council is invariable.

b. A person can be co-opted to the Council, whose duty is to render advice which the council can either take or reject.

The Yabumwura presides over the Traditional Council by virtue of his office as the head of the Gonja State. The Sonyonwura acts in the absence of the Yabumwura.

Outside associations or Youth Associations have no part whatsoever to play in Gonja Traditional matters.

The main festivals of the Traditional area are: *i)* Jintigi, *ii)* Damba, *iii)* Achan, *iv)* Gbandawu, or Yam Festival, *v)* Kuchunufol and *vi)* Dongi.

The relationship between chieftaincy and priesthood in the Ghanaian context is that both are traditional rulers. But whereas the chief is nominated and enstooled or enskinned, the priest is only nominated and his special duty is to serve the gods of the land.

The chiefs are responsible for appointing the Imam/Chief Fetish Priest in their respective areas.

Chiefs used not to obtain permits for any festival, however with inter-tribal mixtures and the institution of Police posts in towns and villages, chiefs do occasionally obtain permits in the case of "Jintigu" or Fire Festival. This is to ensure that natives do not molest strangers.

The Chief normally appoints his gongong beater.

The role of government and arms of government in chieftaincy matters:

> The Prime Minister, the Regional Chief Executive, the Regional Administrative Officer, the District Administrative Officer, and the police.

These arms of government play some role in chieftaincy matters in the way of maintaining peace in times of misunderstandings.

a. Usually a report on the installation of a chief is made to the Government by the Paramount Chief through the Regional House of Chiefs.

b. Government gives recognition to a chief when the Regional House of Chiefs is satisfied with the report on the Chief's installation from the Paramount Chief and passes it to the National House of Chiefs for the chief's title and name to be registered and finally to the Government.

c. A chief need not be gazetted in order to perform the functions of his office. After he has been customarily installed and given recognition by the Yabumwura, it goes without saying that he has the liberty to perform the functions of his office.

d. The police can only step in to maintain law and order when there is a misunderstanding during the installation of a chief.

e. The Government can order seizure of stool or skin properties when the chief concerned contravenes traditional laws or grossly acts against the laws of the country. Skin or stool properties so seized by the Government should remain in the custody of the Paramount Chief.

f. In Gonja, the walking stick or sceptre, the spears, talking drums and the skins (lion-skins) constitute the skin properties.

g. Gonja Tradition does not allow government officials to take skin properties into custody. The Paramount Chief and the divisional chiefs are the rightful custodians of skin properties.

MEMBERSHIP OF THE GONJA TRADITIONAL COUNCIL

The following categories of chiefs form the membership of the council:

1. The Yabumwura—President

a.   The Six Divisional Chiefs

2. The Wasipewura
3. The Kpembewura
4. The Bolewura
5. The Tuluwewura
6. The Kusawguwura
7. The Buipewura

b.   The Eight Elders and the Yabumwura's Nsuawura

8. The Sonyonwura
9. The Damongowura
10. The Choriwura
11. The Debrewura
12. The Mankpanwura
13. The Kulawwura
14. Kpansheguwura
15. Busunuwura
16. The Yabumwura's Nsauwura

c.   The Three Nominated Chiefs from the Various Divisional Areas

Wasipe

17. Yazoriwura Mahama
18. Mankariguwura Dambol
19. Sambonwura Assan

Kpembe

20. Kikpandewura
21. Kanyasewura
22. Kanakulaiwura

Bole

23. Nagbewura Osei
24. Wulasewura Abudu
25. Jamakoro

Tuluwe

26. Bundawura
27. Busunuwura
28. Kajumuwura

Kasawgu

29. Yapeiwura Bakeri
30. Tariwura Wayo
31. Kpankplonsowura Mahama

Buipe

32. Gbungbonsowura
33. Silmawura
34. Danyanpewura

Standing Committee Members

The following were unanimously elected to form the standing Committee: Yabumwura (Chairman), Wasipewura, Kpembewura, Bolewura, Tuluwewura, Kusawguwura, Buipewura, and Damongowura.

Compiled by:
Osafroadu Amankwatia

Submitted by: Tia Adjei, Assistant Registrar to the Northern Regional House of Chiefs. Tamale.

20 November 1973

Appendix I
Gbanya State Legislative Council

We, Musi Buipewura and Mama Yabumwura do hereby state that the following executive councillors and divisional chiefs form the full Gbanya (Gonja) State Council and are empowered to make the laws of the Gbanya State:

Buipewura,	Yabumwura
represented by Kagbapewura	Kpembewura
Sonyonwura	Wasipewura
Debrewura	Bolewura
Mankpanwura	Kungwura
Kula-Wura	Tuluwewura
Choriwura	Kusawguwura
Damongowura	

(Sgd.) Musi Buipewura   His X Mark
(Sgd.) Mama YabumwuraHis X Mark

Before us at Yapei on the 19th May, 1930

(Sgd.) A. Duncan-Johnstone
"   A.W. Cardinal
"   E.F. Burn

Interpreters and Witnesses to Marks.

	His
Kanya Grunshi	X
	Mark

(Sgd.) J.E. Mensah

	His
Adamu Salaga	X
	Mark

Certified true copy
J.R. Turkson

Appendix II
Chiefs Eligible to Succeed
to the Kawulputi of Yabun

We, Musi Buipewura and Mama Yabumwura do hereby state that the five following chiefs are those and those only from whom the Yabumwura is selected:

Kpembewura
Wasipewura (Daboya)
Bolewura
Tuluwewura
Kusawguwura

Signed, Musi Buipewura   His X Mark
Signed, Mama Yabumwura   His X Mark

Before us at Yapei on 19th May, 1930.

(Sgd.) A. Duncan-Johnstone
  "   A.W. Cardinal
  "   E.F. Burn

Interpreters and Witnesses to Marks.

	His
Kanya Grunshi	X
	Mark

(Sgd.) J.W. Mensah

	His
Adamu Salaga	X
	Mark

Certified true copy
J.K. Turkson

Appendix III
Rules of Succession:
Division Chiefs

The rules of succession to the respective Divisional Skins are as follows:

Buipe (Gbipe): Danyanpewura, Gbingbinsiwura, Silmawura are eligible chiefs to succeed and the candidate is appointed by the Kante and Sakpare gates who present the candidate to the Yabumwura for approval before enskinment.

Wasipe: Yazoriwura, who must be a chief from Mamampe and Tikpirpe.

Kpembe: Singbinwura, Kanakulaiwura, and the Kanyasewura succeed in turn, in the order stated.

Bole: Mandarewura, Wulasiwura, Jentilipewura are the eligible chiefs to succeed and the candidate is chosen by the Yabumwura.

Tuluwe: Latepowura, Kajamowura, and the Bondawura succeed in turn.

Kusawgu: Yapeiwura, who must be a son or brother of a Kusawguwura.

The families from which the Divisional Chiefs are appointed are:

The Buipewura is appointed from the gate chiefs of Silima and Gbingbinsi and the three families from which the chiefs are appointed are: 1. Dinkeripe, 2. Lebope, and 3. Danyanpewura.

The Wasipewura is appointed from the following families: 1. Mamape and 2. Tikpiripe. The heir to the skins is appointed to the Yazori skins.

The Kpembewura is appointed from the gate chiefs of the Singbing, Lepo and Kanyase families who bear the titles of Singbingwura, Kanakulaiwura and Kanyasewura (Jawullape) (Kijolobito).

The Bolewura is appointed from three families and they succeed in turn. It is usual for the heir to the Bole skins to be appointed Mandariwura. The families are: 1. Safupe, 2. Jagape, and 3. Denkeripe.

The **Tuluwewura** is appointed from the following families: 1. Latipe and 2. Jawupe. The heir to the skin is usually made the Bundawura.

The **Kusawguwura** is appointed from the following families: 1. Sollepe, 2. Adamape, 3. Jakpape, and 4. Mumunipe. Succession to the skins are in turn. The heir to the skin is usually made Yapei-wura and is appointed by the Yabumwura.

Appendix IV
Rules of Succession:
Binimu (Elders and Councillors)

The rules of succession to the respective skins of the Binimu (Elders and Councillors to the Yabumwura) whose offices are equivalent to those of the Divisional Chiefs, and whose elections/selections must be approved by the Yabumwura are:

Senyonwura is appointed from one family living at Senyon, and the Ewura (Chief cannot come from any other town. Succession is through the male heir, that is, eldest brother, then son. On the death of the Senyonwura the matter is reported to the Yabumwura and he asks the family to elect a successor. The chief is enrobed by the Imam of Dakrupe.

Damongowura is appointed from two branches of the family living in Damongo. These are: 1. Lemupe and 2. Dangape. His election is approved by the Kuntunkurwura (chief drummer) who is the Kasawulwura (priest) and inherits from father to brother, then son.

Debrewura is appointed from the following three gates: 1. Kanyangpe, 2. Kapoasi, and 3. Abrasi. There is no town of Debre, that being the name of the whole area. The chiefs live at Mpaha, Kpabuse or Nasumpe, according to their family.

Mankpangwura is appointed from three branches of the family. The families are: 1. Jakpape and 2. Kugorope. 3. Bangpe.

Kulawwura is appointed from three branches of the family: 1. Jawupe, 2. Chape, and 3. Kabia.

The succession alternates in the above order. The new chief must first be approved by the Aburmasewura and Bolase bi Ewura of Kanyage together with elders called by them. After this the Kafabawura has to approve the candidate and recommend the chief elect to Kpembewura for formal appointment. But note the effect of the enquiry into the constitution and organisation of the Gbanya kingdom, held at Yapei from 17–19 May, 1930.

Appendix V
List of Female Chiefs

The list of Female Chiefs in Gonja is as follows:

Division	Iwurche (Female Chief)	Appointed by
Yabun	Mankuma Wurche	Yabumwura
Gbipe	Maute Wurche	Gbipewura
	Danyangpe Wurche	Gbipewura
Wasipe	Buror Buru Wurche	Wasipewura
	Gbinpe Wurche	"
	Bun Wurche	"
	Buna Wurche	"
	Sei Wurche	"
	Sagya Wurche	"
	Senoari Wurche	"
	Busa Wurche	"
Kpembe	Singbing Wurche	Singbingwura
	Nyolo Wurche	"
	Kpanape Wurche	"
	Dinipo Wurche	Kayansewura
	Kidengi Wurche	"
	Alfai Wurche	"
	Tanche Wurche	"
	Kpenchir Wurche	"
	Longpe Wurche	"
	Chindiri Wurche	Kanakulaiwura
	Leppo Wurche	"
	Jonkombo Wurche	"
	Bosso Wurche	"
	Laba Wurche	"
Bole	Kiape Wurche	Bolewura
	Soma Wurche	"
	Bugai Wurche	"
	Tuna Wurche	"
	Sanjari Wurche	"
	Kasuape Wurche	"
	Kunfusi Wurche	"
	Gbenfu Wurche	"
	Bale Wurche	"
	Darpe (Kulmasa) Wurche	"
	Seripe Wurche	"
	Jilinkon Wurche	"
	Jabori Wurche	"
	Nahari Wurche	"

	Karinson Wurche	"
	Tarinyan Wurche	"
	Gurpe Wurche	"
	Nakwabi Wurche	"
Tuluwe	Tumklan Wurche	Tuluwewura
	Singbin Wurche	"
	Gbemase Wurche	"
	Akoal Wurche	"
	Jasinpewurche	"
Kusawgu	Zou Wurche	Kusawguwura
	Dawale Wurche	"
	Kusawgu Wurche	"
	Yapei Wurche	"
Kpanshegu	Kpanshegu Wurche	Kpansheguwura
	Nom Wurche	"
	Vare Wurche	"
	Chesi Wurche	"
	Jinlo Wurche	"
	Libi Wurche	"
	Zam Wurche	"
Busunu	Busunu Wurche	Busunuwura
	Danbayiri Wurche	"
	Grupe Wurche	"
	Bidima Wurche	"
	Langantere Wurche	"
Sonyon	Sonyonwurche	Sonyonwura
Damongo	Damongo Wurche	Damongowura
	Kasheipe Wurche	"
	Ban Wurche	"
	Budama Wurche	"
Debre	Debre Wurche	"
	Kijaso Wurche	"
	Lanpowrwurche	"
Mankpan	Mankpan Wurche	Mankpanwura
	Wuwato Wurche	"
Kulaw	Silmanchu Wurche	Kalaw-wura
	Kabako Wurche	"
	Kpase Wurche	"
	Boachape Wurche	"
	Akimande Wurche	"

Appendix VI

We, the undersigned Divisional Chiefs of the Gbanya State do hereby acknowledge that we are the subjects of the Yabumwura, and agree to serve him as overlord of Gbanya State from henceforth.

	Their
Soali Kpembewura	X
Abudu Wasipewura	X
Takora Bolewura	X
Kungwura (absent)	
Iddisah Tuluwewura	X
Mama Kusawguwura	X
	Marks

Before us at Yapei in the Kingdom of Gbanya this 19th day of May, 1930.

(Signed) A. Duncan-Johnstone
   "   A.W. Cardinal
   "   E.F. Burn

Interpreters and Witnesses to marks.

	His
Kanyan Grunshi	X
	Mark

(Sgd.)   J.E. Mensah

	His
Adamu Salaga	X
	Mark

Certified true copy.
J.R. Turkson